Student
Grub

EASY RECIPES FOR
TASTY, HEALTHY FOOD

Alastair Williams

STUDENT GRUB

First published in 1991, reprinted 1992 and 1993
Second edition published in 1995
Third edition published in 2000, reprinted 2001 and 2003
Fourth edition published in 2004, reprinted 2006
Fifth edition published in 2008
This edition copyright © Alastair Williams, 2013
All rights reserved.

Summersdale Publishers Ltd
46 West Street
Chichester
West Sussex
PO19 1RP
UK

www.summersdale.com

Printed and bound in China

ISBN: 978-1-84953-413-0

Substantial discounts on bulk quantities of Summersdale books are available to corporations, professional associations and other organisations. For details contact Nicky Douglas by telephone: +44 (0) 1243 756902, fax: +44 (0) 1243 786300 or email: nicky@summersdale.com.

To my parents
with love and thanks

Alastair Williams was a student at numerous establishments of higher education before eventually graduating from Southampton. He has travelled throughout the world in his quest for mouth-watering recipes that can easily be reproduced by any student, and this book is the result.

CONTENTS

Introduction.................6

The Basics..................8

   Conversion Chart...............11

   Glossary of Cooking Terms.......12

   Healthy Eating................14

   Special Diets.................18

   The Store Cupboard............21

   Carbohydrates................23

   Meat........................26

   Fish........................28

   Vegetables..................29

   Spices, Herbs and Seasonings..34

Dressings, Sauces and Dips.........36

Soups and Starters.................44

Side Dishes........................54

Main Dishes........................59

   British......................60

   Italian.....................73

   French......................91

   Oriental....................102

   Indian......................110

   Greek, Turkish and Hungarian...116

   Mexican.....................122

   Spanish.....................125

   American....................129

   Fish........................132

   Salads......................139

Snacks and Midnight Cravings...151

Breakfast Time and Smoothies...160

Cookies and Cakes.....................168

Puddings...................................177

Coffees......................................187

Conclusion.................................191

INTRODUCTION

What's all this cooking stuff about?

Starting University

Higher education is supposed to do more than improve a person academically: time spent at uni will give students an opportunity to experience a wide range of activities and to mature as an adult... well, that's the theory anyway.

Starting uni in new surroundings with new people can be daunting – for those leaving the comfort and security of their home for the first time it may take some getting used to. You'll have to learn to do your own washing and cleaning, and there's no longer a parent's car with a full tank of petrol waiting for you when that emergency trip to A&E/the cinema/the chippy comes up. But it also means you get to enjoy a whole new level of independence and freedom from nagging parents (though we know you love them really!), and there's a host of new and exciting experiences waiting for you around every corner.

Whether you are sharing a house, living in a self-catering flat or in halls of residence, you'll have to feed yourself,

and though mistakes will undoubtedly be made (there's a limit to how many takeaways your stomach – and your student loan – can endure), with the help of this book you'll find out that it can be fun finding your feet in the kitchen.

The recipes and advice in this book will enable you to discover simple but tasty dishes that should still leave you with enough money to get the drinks in afterwards. There are numerous fine cookbooks available that will tell you how to cook dishes such as pigeon breast stuffed with ceps, or how to prepare langoustine drizzled with truffle oil. If that's what you're after, you should put this book down now. The reality of university is that you will want to keep your food spend to a minimum; cooking at uni can be a challenge, but luckily you have this book to guide you on your way.

THE BASICS

What You Need

The chances are that your kitchen, as well as being a health liability, will lack the modern appliances that most family kitchens have. The idea of attempting a meal without a fancy mixer may seem daunting, but it can be done. From personal experience I know that most student kitchens will not even have a set of scales, so many of the measurements given use spoons (tablespoons, teaspoons) and grams (which you can convert into spoons – see Conversion Chart).

You may also need patience. Many of the recipes given are quick and simple, but when attempting something more adventurous it is essential not to give up. There are going to be times when your soufflé looks more like a pancake, but even the best chefs have the occasional disaster.

Some people will find cooking very easy, but it's not everyone's forte. The rest of us mere mortals need a little more perseverance and patience. Cooking disasters are all part of the fun, and experimenting with this book could lead to all sorts of wonderful experiences, some of which may even be of a culinary nature.

If you have had no experience of cooking (and judging from some of my friends who lived for three years on baked beans and toast, without the wit even to combine the two, this is entirely possible) then you will need some help. Unfortunately, most cookery books tend to contain far too many irrelevant, expensive, impractical and unpalatable recipes for students. What would your housemates think if you were to serve them a platter of marinated pigs' trotters? Rest assured there are no monkey brains or goats' testicles to be found in this book. Much like in a restaurant, it is the quality of food, the friendliness of the service and the general ambience that can provide a perfect meal – not frilly tablecloths, crystal glasses and extortionate prices.

Common Sense

The recipes in this book are designed with simplicity in mind, both in terms of implements and cooking skills required. All that is needed is common sense. All cooking times and heats are approximate. Cooking is an instinctive thing and no number of instructions can replace common sense and initiative. Before you try any recipe, read it through first to make sure you have all the ingredients and equipment as well as the time to prepare it.

Health and Safety

If you are in a large shared house, the kitchen may have to cope with as many as seven, eight or nine people. It is quite easy when there are large numbers of people sharing a small kitchen for it to become quite disgusting. Having been a student for a number of years I have had the opportunity to visit many student kitchens, and most of them were truly revolting – the washing up was normally only done when there were no more spare plates or cutlery available, or when parents or landlords came to visit.

It is a good idea if you are in a shared house to organise some sort of rota for cooking and cleaning. If one or two people cook each night for everyone it avoids the hassle that would occur if everybody in the house waited to use the cooker for themselves. It also means that you will only be cooking perhaps once or twice a week.

Once you have established that your cooking environment is clean and hygienic pay special attention to the instructions for food storage. All perishable foodstuff will have a sell-by date printed on its packaging, and clear instructions on how long it can languish in your fridge before it needs to be eaten/disposed of. This is especially important when it comes to meat and dairy products. Frozen foods need to be kept hard frozen until you start cooking them. If food is defrosted it must be cooked and cooled before refreezing. Warm food should not be placed directly into a fridge – wait for it to cool down first. And remember, food left lying around for long enough will go off and harmful bacteria will grow – even an hour or two is enough for food to start going off. If the green furry parts in your kitchen make it look more like a biology experiment than a hygienic place suitable for food storage and preparation, it might be a good idea to clear the whole kitchen and disinfect it.

CONVERSION CHART

The recipes in this book are given in metric measurements, which are self-explanatory, but many small amounts are measured in terms of spoons or cups.

The following abbreviations are used:

tbsp = tablespoon (the one that's too big to put in your mouth)
tsp = teaspoon (what you put in your teacup)

Spoon measures can also be substituted for grams with certain ingredients, which is handy for those without a set of kitchen scales. Obviously the weights of all ingredients will vary, but here are some rough measures:

1 tbsp = 25 g of… syrup, jam, honey, etc.
2 tbsp = 25 g of… butter, sugar

3 tbsp = 25 g of… cornflour, cocoa, custard, flour
4 tbsp = 25 g of… grated cheese, porridge oats

All spoon measures refer to level spoons, not heaped.
1 cup of rice weighs roughly 200 g

In all recipes the oven should be heated to the temperature stated prior to cooking to allow it to warm up. Ovens vary but as a rule of thumb Celsius is roughly half the Fahrenheit temperature.
   Set fan-assisted ovens 25 degrees Celsius (approximately 50 degrees Fahrenheit) lower than others and reduce cooking time by 10 minutes for every hour of cooking time.

GLOSSARY OF COOKING TERMS

Baste
To spoon fat or oil over food to keep it moist. Usually done to a joint of meat whilst it is in the oven.

Beat
This is the mixing of ingredients using a wooden spoon, a fork or a whisk.

Chop
To cut into small pieces.

Cream
To mix fat with another ingredient like sugar until it becomes creamy.

Dice
To cut into small cubes.

Grate
A grater can produce coarse or fine shavings of food, such as cheese or vegetables.

Knead
To use your knuckles to smooth dough out, the idea being to get a smooth texture.

Marinade
A combination of juices, spices and oils in which meat is soaked to enhance the flavour.

Parboil
This is the partial boiling of something. The cooking of the food will then normally be finished off by another method, e.g. roasting potatoes.

Peel
To remove the skin or the outer layer of a vegetable.

Rub in
To rub flour and fat together between your fingertips until they resemble breadcrumbs.

Simmer

To cook just below the boiling point, so that only an occasional bubble appears on the surface.

Steam

One of the healthiest ways to prepare vegetables, while ensuring they keep their crunch. Steamers are widely and cheaply available in different styles, or you can use a makeshift one by placing the veg in a colander and resting above a pan of boiling water, with a lid on top.

Stir-fry

Healthier and quicker than frying, and also uses less oil so is cheaper! Great for oriental dishes and for retaining the goodness of the veg.

Top and tail

To cut off the drier, knobbly ends of vegetables such as carrots, leeks, sweet potatoes etc.

TOP TIP

To cut down on the amount of oil used in recipes, it's worth investing in heavy-based, non-stick cookware, and using an oil spray which provides a thin coating.

HEALTHY EATING

Healthy eating is something that many of us pay little thought to – youthful decadence is more fun, after all. But if your idea of a balanced diet means equal amounts of food to alcohol you should read this section.

Normally, when living at home and eating three square meals a day (presumably including plenty of vegetables and fruit), you will receive all the vitamins and minerals needed to stay healthy. All this can change when you go away to uni. It is very easy to start skipping meals – most people I knew who lived in halls very rarely had breakfast, took only a sandwich or some chocolate for a quick, filling lunch, and then perhaps a jacket potato with chips for dinner. This is not particularly healthy.

Those living in a shared house will find cooking easier than those living on their own: you can take turns to cook, and it is much easier and more enjoyable cooking for a group than for just one. If you are living on your own try inviting friends or a neighbour over so that you can share meals with them. Cooking for one is less efficient and less economical, and it can be hard to put in much effort.

Eating food does much more than fill your belly. It provides the energy for movement, allows the healing of wounds and instigates the production of protoplasm which helps to replace dead cells.

If you want to stay healthy you must have a balanced diet. There are certain things that are essential to obtaining this.

Carbohydrates

These are the provider of energy. They also happen to be the cheapest types of food and can be found in things like

potatoes, bread and rice. Although these foods are always available in ample supply, take care to limit your own intake because an excess of carbohydrates leads to obesity.

Fats

These also provide energy for the body, but they take longer to digest than carbohydrates. This means they are useful for storing energy. There are two main types of fats: saturated and unsaturated. Saturated fat can lead to heart disease, diabetes and high blood pressure, and should only be consumed in moderation – it is present in dairy products like butter, margarine, milk, cheese and, of course, in meat. Unsaturated fat is good for you, helping the body absorb nutrients and providing energy – this can be found in avocados, nuts, lean meat, olives and fish.

Proteins

The word protein derives from the Greek word 'of first importance', and that is exactly what they are. Proteins are necessary for bodily development

and repairs to damaged cells. Proteins are found in fish, lean meat, vegetables, grains, beans, nuts, seeds, soy products, milk, cheese and eggs.

Vitamins

This is one area where many students fail to supply the correct amounts vital to keeping the body in perfect running order. The following is a list of the most essential vitamins and their sources:

Vitamin A

Vitamin A is present in dairy products like cheese, eggs and milk, and in green vegetables, fish and liver.

Vitamin B

Vitamin B is made up of more than 10 different vitamins. They are to be found in wholegrain cereals, liver, yeast. lean meat, beans, peas and nuts.

Vitamin C

In the days of Nelson, scurvy was a common problem for a ship's crew. This is a disease resulting from a lack of vitamin C. The main source of the vitamin is citrus fruits like lemons and oranges, and blackcurrants and fresh vegetables. Vitamin C is great for the immune system and helps to protect against the common cold.

Vitamin D

Vitamin D is essential for the absorption of calcium to take place. A deficiency in calcium can lead to rickets in children, which means the bones are weak. In adults it can result in bow legs. The main source of Vitamin D is sunlight, but this can be in pretty short supply throughout much of the year – especially if you are holed up in a lecture theatre, the library or the pub! Luckily it can also be found in milk, butter, cheese, fish and liver.

Vitamin E

This is a vitamin that does not usually pose a deficiency problem in our society. It is found in vegetables such as avocados, tomatoes, spinach and watercress; blackberries, mangoes, nuts, wholegrains, olive oil, mackerel and salmon.

Vitamin K

This is found in green vegetables and wholegrain cereals. It helps the blood clotting process.

Roughage (aka dietary fibre)

This is vital if you want to have a healthily functioning digestive system and avoid constipation. High-fibre cereals and fruit and vegetables provide good sources of roughage.

Water

It may seem obvious that the body requires a substantial amount of water to function, but in case you forget this is a reminder.

Minerals

There are three main minerals whose continued supply can all too easily be jeopardised: iron, calcium and iodine. Other minerals such as the phosphates, potassium, magnesium and sodium are generally in good supply.

Iron

This is vital for the formation of the red blood cells. If a person has a deficiency of iron it can lead to anaemia (a shortage of red blood cells). Ensuring a high iron intake is not as simple as eating a bag of nails, however. Far better to eat liver, which is slightly more palatable, and is an excellent source of iron, as are other meats, dried herbs, seeds and dark green leafy vegetables.

Calcium

This mineral is important for strong bones and teeth. It is found in dairy products like milk, butter and cheese, tofu and soya products and green leafy vegetables.

Iodine

Iodine, although important, is not needed in the same quantities as calcium or iron. Fish, milk, yogurt and seaweed are good sources of iodine.

Supplements

A healthy, balanced diet should give you all the vitamins and minerals you need, but if you choose to supplement your diet with them in pill form it is important to follow the recommended dosage, and to consult your doctor if you have any questions or concerns.

SPECIAL DIETS

There are going to be occasions when you might need to cater for a friend who has special dietary requirements. This could be due to their health needs, their belief system, or simply their personal choice. There would be too many variations to cover all eventualities and there are plenty of specific recipe books available that cater for even the most unusual of diets, but here is a basic introduction to some of the most common requirements.

Gluten-Free Diet

A gluten-free diet is essential for people who have coeliac disease or dermatitis herpetiformis (a gluten-induced skin sensitivity). Coeliacs suffer from a reaction to gluten, a protein that is found in wheat, rye, barley and, usually, oats.
A gluten-free diet involves the complete avoidance of all foods made from the above. This means that cakes, biscuits, pasta and noodles, for instance, are all forbidden, unless you obtain specially made gluten-free versions (these are available in health-food shops and larger supermarkets). For more information on coeliac disease take a look at the Coeliac Society website: http://www.coeliac. co.uk

Dairy-Free Diet

Someone who suffers a reaction to lactose is referred to as lactose intolerant. It means that they are unable to break down the sugar called lactose that is found in milk. Lactose intolerance can vary in its severity. Some sufferers are intolerant to all dairy products including eggs; others only have a reaction to certain dairy products. If you are catering for someone with a lactose intolerance, you should steer clear of all dairy products, such as milk, cream, crème fraîche, soured cream and yogurt. Many manufactured products will have to be avoided too. Cakes, biscuits and ready-meals are all likely to contain dairy products.

For more information see: http://www.lactose.co.uk

Vegetarian, Pescetarian or Vegan?

A lacto-ovo vegetarian is someone who excludes meat and fish from their diet, but eats dairy products and eggs.

A pescetarian is someone who excludes meat from their diet, but eats fish and seafood, dairy products and eggs.

A vegan is someone who eats no animal products at all, so they will exclude meat, fish, seafood, dairy products, eggs and honey from their diet.

If you are catering for a vegetarian, pescetarian or vegan friend, there are plenty of meat and dairy substitutes available in larger supermarkets and health-food shops, which are very tasty – you might discover some new and interesting foods!

Religious Dietary Requirements

Islam

Muslims will not eat pork. They will only eat meat if it has been prepared in the Halal manner, which means that the animal is slaughtered by slitting the throat and allowing its blood to drain away. Muslims are also prohibited from drinking alcohol.

Buddhism

Most Buddhists practise vegetarianism as they believe in abstaining from the harming of all living beings.

Judaism

There are several different dietary restrictions in the Jewish faith, although the extent to which they are followed may vary. They will only eat meat which adheres to the rules of kosher, which means it must be from an animal that 'chews the cud and has a cloven hoof', and fish must have both scales and fins. This means they must not eat the meat of a pig, or shellfish, amongst other things.

Hinduism

Most Hindus are vegetarian or vegan, and many will not eat onion or garlic or other foods with strong flavours. Cows are regarded as sacred, and pigs as unclean, which means that no meat from a cow or pig will be included in their diet.

TOP TIP

100 g of tofu provides roughly a quarter of your daily calcium needs, and plenty of protein, iron and other minerals.

THE STORE CUPBOARD

It is a common problem when cooking that whatever ingredients you have in your cupboard will always be the things you don't need, while whatever you do need will be conspicuous by its absence. You will also find that certain things in your cupboard will disappear almost immediately, like choccy biscuits, whilst Grandma's home-made chutney will stay lurking in the depths of the cupboard until you change house, or until the contents of the jar are used as a loose floor-tile adhesive.

Here is a suggested list of useful things to have in your cupboard:

Cans

Apart from the obligatory cans of lager, canned food is always useful for its longevity, and whole meals can often be prepared from one can.

Examples:

- Baked beans
- Chick peas
- Coconut milk
- Kidney beans
- Lentils
- Soups
- Sweetcorn
- Tomatoes (used consistently throughout this book)
- Tuna

Dried fruits

- Apple rings
- Apricots
- Banana chips
- Dates
- Sultanas, currants and raisins

THE BASICS

Flour

- Plain
- Self-raising

Nuts

- Almonds
- Cashew nuts
- Walnuts

Oils:

- Olive
- Sunflower
- Vegetable

Pasta

Choose from the long, thin kind (spaghetti, tagliatelle) or the huge variety of shaped pasta (such as conchiglie, penne, fusilli)

Rice

- Basmati
- Long grain

Sugars

- Brown
- Caster
- Granulated or golden granulated
- Icing

CARBOHYDRATES

Carbs should form the basis of most of your meals – they release energy slowly, making you feel a lot fuller and more alert than if you had opted to scoff a few chocolate bars instead before that lecture!

Rice

There are various types of rice available, but if you are trying to stretch out your loan then buy the cheapest. Allow about 50 to 75 g per person. If you don't have any scales, a cup holds about 200 g, so use that as a guideline.

Before cooking rice it is advisable to put it in a sieve and wash it. This removes some of the starch and will help to prevent it from sticking. After washing the rice, place it in a saucepan with a covering of water and cook according to the instructions on the packet. Make sure there is enough water that it won't burn on the bottom, and cover with a lid. The time it takes depends on the type of rice used. The best way of testing it is to taste it. If it is still hard in the middle it needs a bit longer.

Pasta

Pasta comes in a wide range of shapes and sizes, perhaps the most common being spaghetti. You can buy fresh pasta (as a friend commented, 'that soggy stuff in a packet') which tastes great but is not so cheap as the dried variety, and doesn't last very long. For those who have not outgrown tinned pasta you might be lucky enough to get space invaders, but I don't think that the Italians would approve.

You should allow roughly 50 g of pasta per person. After the water has boiled add a pinch of salt. Long pasta like spaghetti should be eased gently into a pan making sure that it is not broken. Adding a couple of drops of olive oil to the heated water can prevent the pasta sticking. The pasta should be cooked with the lid off, and stirred occasionally.

Normally, dried pasta requires 8 to 10 minutes in boiling water, but the packaging for each type will give you the correct cooking time, as different shapes do require different times. Someone once told me that the best way to see if it is cooked is to throw a piece on the wall. If it sticks, it's ready. Apart from making a mess on your wall this is not the most reliable way to test the pasta. While it should have some 'bite' to it (al dente), make sure that the pasta is not undercooked as this could result in indigestion.

If you are cooking fresh pasta it normally only requires 2 or 3 minutes, so watch it carefully. If you overcook your pasta it will stick together and will taste very doughy.

Potatoes

Chips, crisps, mash – need I say more about the versatility of this deceptively plain-looking discovery of Sir Walter?

Here are some guidelines for cooking the perfect tater.

There are two basic types of potato: new and old. Both are available all year round, with new potatoes traditionally served boiled as a side to meat dishes or cold as a salad, and 'old' potatoes being the common type used in most other recipes – suitable for mashing, baking, chipping etc. Judge the amount of potatoes per person by imagining how they will look on your plate.

All potatoes need to scrubbed before cooking, and peeled if you are chipping or mashing. Skins can be left on new potatoes, and other dishes can be tastier if you leave the skin on the veg. Clearly the clue is in the name with jacket potatoes.

There are many different ways in which you can cook potatoes. The most common way is to boil them. After peeling or scrubbing the potatoes, cut into halves or quarters, depending on their size, then place in salted boiling water for 15 to 20 minutes or until they are tender all the way through. If you want mashed potato make sure they are well cooked otherwise they will be lumpy. Drain the potatoes, add a knob of butter and a drop of milk (or olive oil if you prefer not to use dairy), then using a potato masher squash until they are nice and creamy, adding more milk and some black pepper if desired.

If you want to prepare a more exotic mash, you can add a teaspoon of smooth French mustard and some finely chopped fresh rosemary.

Roast Potatoes

Peel the potatoes, then halve or quarter them depending on their size. Parboil (this means they are only partially boiled) for 5 minutes in salted boiling water, then drain. Shaking the potatoes briefly in the saucepan at this stage will give them nice fluffy edges. Place the semi-cooked potatoes in a baking tray with some oil and stick in the oven on Gas Mark 6 (200 °C, 400 °F) near the top of the oven if possible. Baste the potatoes with the oil a couple times while they are cooking. Roast the potatoes until they are golden and verging on crispiness; this should take between 60 and 90 minutes.

Chips

These things are almost a British institution, and they should of course be served with fish and wrapped in an old newspaper with lashings of vinegar and salt. If that description hasn't quelled your craving for chips then here is how to make your own.

Peel some old potatoes and cut into chip shapes. If you are feeling sophisticated slice them more thinly into French fries. The healthiest method is to place the potatoes on a baking tray and drizzle oil over them (tossing them to coat), then bake for 45 to 50 minutes. The alternative to oven baking is to deep fry them: this is potentially dangerous so take care. The chips need to be covered or at least partially covered in oil to cook, so a large amount of oil is needed.

Heat the oil in a large frying pan, then carefully add the chips, taking care not to throw them in the pan, otherwise hot oil will be splashed.

Fry the chips until they are crisp, making sure that the oil does not get too hot.

Whatever you do, remember to turn the heat off. If your fat does catch fire it is imperative that you do the right thing (see health and safety, p.10).

MEAT

Vegetarians can skip this section, but those carnivores out there can now indulge in mental images of fillet steak and Sunday roasts. Although the price can be beyond the budget of some students, chicken is still relatively inexpensive, and certain cuts of red meats (and that doesn't just include the offal) shouldn't break the bank.

Beef

When choosing a piece of beef it should be a light red colour and slightly elastic, with not too much gristle (but if it contains no gristle at all it will have a poor flavour).

There are many different cuts of beef, and each is suitable for different methods of cooking:

Roasting

- Topside
- Ribs
- Rump

Grilling or Frying

- Fillet
- Rump
- Entrecôte
- Minced

Stewing

- Brisket
- Flank
- Chuck

Chicken

When buying chicken it should smell fresh and the flesh should be firm. Chicken is very versatile: most parts can be fried, roasted, stewed, etc.

Pork

Pork is cheaper than beef and should be a pale red colour. It is important when preparing pork that it is cooked through sufficiently; the danger in eating undercooked pork is that tapeworms can take a fancy to your stomach. The meat should be white, not pink, after cooking.

Roasting

- Loin
- Leg
- Blade-bone

Grilling or Frying

- Chops
- Ribs
- Loin

Lamb

Lamb should be a pinkish red colour, and the bones at the joints should be red.

Roasting

- Shoulder
- Leg

- Best end of neck
- Loin

Grilling

- Liver

Stewing

- Loin
- Leg
- Breast
- Liver

Sausages

The usual methods for cooking sausages are frying or grilling. For those who want to minimise the relative unhealthiness of the sausage, grilling or barbecuing is the better way to choose.

To fry: heat some oil in a frying pan, and fry the sausages for 15 to 20 minutes. Turn them regularly when cooking to make sure they brown and cook evenly.

To grill: leave under the grill for about 10 minutes on each side, on a medium heat.

FISH

If a recipe uses a whole fish it will need cleaning. This does not mean give it a bubble bath – it means the head, gills and innards have to be removed. Normally fish come already 'cleaned', but, if they don't, ask the fishmonger to do it for you.

Choosing fish is important. Look for the following qualities:

(i) It should not smell.

(ii) The eyes should be bright and full. If the fish is not so fresh the eyes will be dull.

(iii) The gills should be slime-free, clean and shiny.

(iv) If you poke a fresh fish, the flesh will spring back up.

Frozen fish does not tend to have as full a flavour as fresh fish. It is, however, useful to keep a couple of cod fillets in the freezer as they can be cooked fairly quickly and easily.

VEGETABLES

It's all too easy to leave out vegetables from a low-budget diet: students often fail to balance their diet in this respect. The only vegetable with which they are familiar is usually the 'couch potato'.

Prepared to mend your ways? Rather than sticking with humdrum peas and carrots, try experimenting with some more exciting vegetables.

Below is a list of some of the common and not-so-common vegetables available in most supermarkets, explaining how they should be prepared and various ways of cooking them.

Asparagus

These green spears can be steamed, boiled, grilled or used in stir-fries. For best results steam for a few minutes and serve with butter and pepper. It is best to buy asparagus seasonally as otherwise it can be very expensive.

Aubergine

Also known as 'eggplant'. Cut the top and bottom off and then slice thinly. Sprinkle lightly with salt and leave for 10 minutes. Before cooking, rinse the slices in water. A common method for cooking aubergines is to fry them until they soften, although they are also excellent baked or grilled.

Baby sweetcorn

The only preparation needed is washing, following which they can be gently boiled, steamed or stir-fried. To benefit from their full flavour they need to retain their crispness.

Beans (French)

Wash them and top and tail. Cut into 3 cm lengths, or leave whole. Place in boiling water with a little salt and cook for 10 to 15 minutes. Delicious as they stand, or, for a bit of pizzazz, they can be tossed in butter or oil and herbs.

Broccoli

Wash in cold water, cut off the stalks then divide into florets. Cook in salted boiling water for about 7 minutes. It is important not to overcook broccoli because it will go mushy and lose most of its flavour.

Brussels sprouts

Remove the outer leaves and cut a cross into the base, then wash in cold water. Steam or cook in salted boiling water for about 10 minutes.

Cabbage

There are three main varieties of cabbage: green, white and red. Remove the tough outer leaves and the centre stalk. You can either shred the leaves or perhaps quarter them. To cook the shredded cabbage either steam or place in boiling water for a few minutes until it's tender and ready to eat (this will be longer for green and white cabbage than red).

Carrots

Top and tail the carrots and then either using a peeler or a knife peel off the skin. Before cooking they can be quartered or sliced. Baby carrots can be cooked whole. Cook in boiling water for about 15 minutes. Carrots can be eaten raw in salads, etc. They can also be roasted in oil when cooking a roast dinner.

Cauliflower

Wash in cold water and then divide into florets. Steam or cook in salted boiling water until tender – this should take about 10 minutes, depending on the size of the florets. Cauliflower can also be eaten raw and used for crudités at parties.

Courgettes

Having been force-fed these things for years I have almost come to like them. First of all give them a wash, then top and tail them. Slice thinly and steam, oven roast or fry in butter or oil for about 10 minutes.

Garlic

This strong-smelling bulb is a kitchen staple, used liberally throughout this book. It adds a delicious flavour to almost any kind of dish, and pairs up well with onion and mushrooms – and is a great addition to any Italian dish.

Leeks

Remove the top dark green bit and the roots and wash. They can either be sliced into rings, quartered or even left whole. To cook either steam, boil for 10 to 15 minutes or fry in oil or butter for about 10 minutes.

Mangetout

If you haven't seen these before, they look like pea pods that have been squashed by a lorry. But they taste delicious and are almost worth the extortionate amount you will be charged for them.

To prepare your mangetout, wash and top and tail them. If boiling them, they need only 3 or 4 minutes because they maintain their flavour better when still crisp. They can also be fried gently in butter or oil for a few minutes until they soften slightly. They make a colourful addition in a stir-fry.

Mushrooms

It might be tempting to save that student loan by picking your own wild mushrooms, but this can be very dangerous (even if you think you're sure it's not poisonous, you should always ask an expert before eating any!) and should not be seen as an alternative to buying them at the supermarket or greengrocers.

Once you have bought your mushrooms, wipe them with a clean cloth to remove any dirt. Either remove or trim the stalk and then slice or leave whole. The mushrooms can be fried or grilled. To fry, heat a little oil or butter in a frying pan and cook for about 3 to 4 minutes, depending on size. To grill, put under a hot grill with a light covering of butter.

Onions

The best way to stop your eyes watering when chopping onions is to get someone else to do it. Top and tail the onion first, then peel off the outer layer. It can be chopped or sliced into rings. Onions are normally fried in oil for about 5 minutes.

Peas

The most common way of buying peas is in the frozen form, but if you buy fresh ones (i.e. still in the pod), you need to shell them and wash them in cold water first. Either way, place them in boiling water for about 10 minutes to cook.

Parsnips

Top and tail, then peel and chop into largish pieces or thick slices. They can be boiled, fried or roasted.

To boil, place in boiling water with a pinch of salt for about 20 minutes or until they are tender.

If they are to be fried they need to be cut into thin slices or chips, otherwise they will not cook all the way through. Perhaps the nicest way of cooking parsnips is to bake them. Place the parsnips in an ovenproof dish with a couple of tablespoons of oil and bake in a hot oven for about 40 minutes. They can be basted as if they were roast potatoes.

Peppers

The most commonly available peppers are the red and green ones, although there are yellow and orange varieties. They all have different flavours – the lighter in colour they are the sweeter they are, so the yellow ones are the sweetest and the green ones the most bitter.

Top and tail, then core and remove all the seeds. Slice into rings then halve and fry in a little oil for 5 minutes or so. They can also be eaten raw and are particularly nice in salads.

Potatoes

See Carbohydrates (p.23).

Pumpkin

If you have a whole pumpkin, cut into quarters then remove all the seeds and pulp from the inside. Remove the skin and cut into chunks. To boil, place in salted boiling water for about 30 minutes.

After the pumpkin has been boiled it can be fried in butter for 5 minutes. Alternatively, dice the vegetable and lightly coat the chunks in vegetable or olive oil and roast them in the oven.

Spinach

The magic green weed that did wonders for Popeye hasn't yet had much effect on me! When buying spinach, buy more than you would if it was cabbage, as spinach will shrink considerably during cooking. Discard any yellowed leaves, then place in a small amount of boiling water for about 5 minutes. Frozen spinach is a quick and easy way of enjoying this iron-rich vegetable. Grated nutmeg and spinach taste good together.

Sweet potato

This makes a nice alternative to ordinary potatoes and can be prepared in the same way to make roast potatoes or mash. When making mash, add butter and black pepper.

Sweetcorn

Remove the husks and the ends, then place in boiling water for 10 minutes. Drain and serve with butter and fresh black pepper.

Tomatoes

Fresh tomatoes can be fried or grilled or eaten raw in salads. For use in cooking, the best and cheapest option is to buy tinned chopped tomatoes. However, if a recipe calls for you to skin fresh tomatoes (e.g. in a sauce or soup), place them in a large pan of boiling water for about a minute. Remove from the hot water and instantly transfer to cold water to cool. The skins should now come away easily.

SPICES, HERBS AND SEASONINGS

Given moderate use, these can transform a plain-tasting meal into something special. Just remember the amounts used have to be carefully controlled, the idea being to enhance the flavour of the food, not to annihilate your taste buds.

When a recipe includes 'salt and pepper' it generally means a pinch of each, but it is up to the individual to season according to taste. One of the most essential items in a kitchen should be a pepper mill. Freshly ground pepper tastes so much better than the stuff that is pre-ground, so try to get hold of one. Here are the most commonly used spices, herbs and seasonings:

Basil

Bay leaves

Black pepper

Capers

Caraway seeds

Cayenne seeds

Chillies

Chilli powder

Chutney

Chives

Cinnamon

Cloves

Curry powder

Essences

Flavourings

Garlic

Garam masala

Lemon juice

Mace

Marjoram

Mint

Mustard (French or English)

Nutmeg

Oregano

Parsley

Paprika pepper

Rosemary

Sage

Salt

Soy sauce

Sweet and sour sauce

Tabasco sauce

Thyme

Vinegar (cider, malt or wine)

Worcestershire sauce

TOP TIP

If a recipe calls for fresh herbs and you only have dried, or the other way around, as a general rule you only need ⅓ of the amount of dried herbs.

DRESSINGS, SAUCES AND DIPS

The use of sauces and dressings can provide an exciting accompaniment to many otherwise plain-tasting dishes.

WHITE SAUCES

There are lots of variations of white sauces which can be used with a large number of dishes. You could even try making your own! They all start with a basic roux.

Ingredients

50 g of butter
50 g of plain flour
500 ml of milk

Melt the butter in a small saucepan, but don't let it brown. Then stir in the flour and cook gently for a couple of minutes, trying to avoid getting any lumps. This is called a roux.

Remove the roux from the heat and add a little of the milk. It has to be added gradually otherwise it will end up being lumpy. Stir in small amounts of milk at a time until a smooth consistency is achieved. When all the milk has been added return the pan to the heat to thicken.

Variations:

Cheese Sauce

Add 100 g of grated cheese to the white sauce when you return it to the heat. Simmer for five minutes or so, then season with salt and pepper to taste. This can be used for cauliflower cheese and lasagne, and other pasta dishes.

Parsley Sauce

Add 4 tbsp of chopped fresh parsley, and salt and pepper to taste, just before serving. This goes especially well with fish dishes.

DRESSINGS, SAUCES AND DIPS

FRENCH DRESSING

There are many variations of French dressing, and most people have their own favourite combinations. Olive oil is a must for an authentic-tasting dressing – vegetable oil, although much cheaper, will not taste as good. Here are a few ideas...

Ingredients

Olive oil

Wine vinegar

Seasonings of your choice

It is unlikely that you are going to need vast quantities of the stuff so as a guideline use 4 parts olive oil to 1 part wine vinegar. A dash of French mustard, pepper, oregano or lemon juice can be added for more flavour. Place all the ingredients together in a small screw-top jar, and shake to combine the flavours.

YOGURT DRESSING

Great for cooling the palate when eating spicy dishes.

Ingredients

125 ml of plain yogurt

1 tbsp of lemon juice

Salt

Pepper

Mix the yogurt and lemon juice together. Season according to taste.

MAYONNAISE

A staple on British dinner tables – great in a burger or on chips.

Ingredients

2 egg yolks

1 tsp of smooth French mustard

300 ml of olive oil

2 tsp of white wine vinegar

Squirt of lemon juice

Salt

Pepper

Put the egg yolks into a mixing bowl with the mustard and mix together. Slowly begin to add the olive oil. The main problem with making mayonnaise is that it can curdle if the oil is added too quickly. Mayonnaise is time-consuming to make, but it is essential to take care. A fine drizzle of oil is needed and has to be controlled with total precision. Hold the bottle of oil at the bottom in the palm of your hand, as this gives more control. Using a balloon whisk, beat the yolks and the oil together. You will notice that the colour is quite yellow in comparison with the bought variety, but this is the way it should be. Keep whisking the mayonnaise until all the oil is added, then add the vinegar, lemon juice and seasoning, and mix together. Taste and adjust the flavourings to suit.

Mayonnaise can be produced in a food processor, but again fine control is required and the result is not as good. Put all the ingredients, bar the oil, in the processor and switch on, then add the oil slowly.

PESTO

This recipe uses insane quantities of fresh basil, and the aroma is intoxicating. Pesto is traditionally served with pasta, but it can also be spread on toast or in a sandwich, drizzled over chicken or used as a salad dressing.

Ingredients

2 cloves of garlic

2 cups of fresh basil leaves

50 g of pine nuts

3 tbsp of Parmesan

125 ml of olive oil

Salt

Peel and crush the garlic cloves. Put the garlic, basil leaves and pine nuts in a blender and grind for a few seconds. Then add the grated cheese, oil and salt and mix well. If you are a stickler for authenticity, then you should prepare the pesto in a mortar, but a blender is far quicker.

HUMMUS

This one is a dip that can be served with freshly chopped vegetables (crudités) or pitta bread. Although hummus is available ready-made, it is cheaper to make your own. Having said that, I find it easier to use canned chick peas instead of soaking dried ones for hours. Note that a blender is needed for this recipe.

Ingredients

2 cloves of garlic

1 can of chickpeas

Juice of 1 lemon

2 tbsp of olive oil

100 g of natural unsweetened yogurt

½ tsp of ground cumin

Peel and chop the garlic. Put all the ingredients in a blender and let them have it! Switch off when a soft consistency is achieved. Then put in a dish and chill for an hour or two.

CUCUMBER RAITA

If the roof of your mouth is feeling like a furnace after a hot curry, this might help. Cucumber raita is very refreshing and simple to prepare.

Ingredients

½ cucumber

1 small pot of natural yogurt

1 tbsp of olive oil

1 tbsp of mint

Salt

Pepper

Peel the cucumber and chop into small pieces. Mix the cucumber, yogurt and chopped mint together in a bowl, pour the oil on top, and season.

SOUPS AND STARTERS

Also known (though not in student circles) as entrées and hors d'oeuvres. Guaranteed at first to shock your dinner guests into thinking that you have been somewhat frugal with the grub, it is important to emphasise that this is only a starter, so that they realise the extent of your sophistication.

These dishes are obviously intended for special occasions, and are not designed to fit in with the typical weekly budget. But the soup recipes can make a filling meal in themselves, and simply by increasing the portions some of the other recipes can be served as main dishes.

GARLIC BREAD

This has to be another classic student recipe, though if you had been planning a romantic evening you might want to make sure you both eat it so one of you doesn't have smellier breath than the other!

Ingredients

150 g of butter

2 cloves of garlic

1 stick of French bread

Put the butter in a small mixing bowl. It helps if the butter is soft. Peel and finely chop the garlic and add to the butter, mixing well with a fork. Slice the French stick at 4 cm intervals, without actually severing it, and spread some of the butter on both sides of each slit. Then close up the gaps and wrap the loaf in foil. Place in the oven and cook for 15 to 20 minutes at Gas Mark 5 (190 °C, 375 °F).

MUSHROOMS WITH GARLIC BUTTER

Garlic again... well, you either love it or hate it.

Ingredients

100 g of mushrooms

100 g of butter

2 cloves of garlic

Remove the stalks of the mushrooms and wipe off any dirt. Peel and finely chop the garlic, and mix together with the butter. Now you can either fry the mushrooms in the melted garlic butter, or mix the whole lot together and bake in the oven for 15 minutes at Gas Mark 5 (190 °C, 375 °F).

MINI SAUSAGES WITH HONEY AND ROSEMARY

This has to be one of my favourite dishes – just writing about it makes me drool! Fresh rosemary is a must, though.

Ingredients

Pack of mini sausages

3 tbsp of runny honey

Handful of fresh rosemary

Arrange the sausages in a baking dish, spoon on the honey, then place the rosemary on top. Bake in the oven at Gas Mark 6 (200°C, 400 °F) for about 25 minutes, turning occasionally so they brown evenly.

GAZPACHO

This is a thin, chilled soup that is very refreshing on a hot summer's evening. A blender is needed for this recipe. I often add a dash of Tabasco sauce, but this is optional.

Ingredients

225 g of ripe tomatoes

½ green pepper

½ red pepper

1 cucumber

1 onion

1 clove of garlic

2 slices of day-old bread

600 ml of tomato juice

2 tbsp of olive oil

1 tbsp of sherry vinegar

1 tbsp of fresh parsley

Salt

Pepper

Skin the tomatoes (see Vegetables section, p.29). Chop the peppers, cucumber, onion, garlic and tomatoes, and put aside a little of each for the garnish. Whizz the bread in the blender to create breadcrumbs. Place all the ingredients except for the oil and seasoning into the blender for 2 minutes or so. Then add the remaining ingredients, and place in the fridge for at least 3 hours. A few ice cubes can be added to speed up this process, but don't add too many as it will dilute the flavour of the soup. Serve with the reserved vegetables on top.

CARROT AND GINGER SOUP

SERVES 4

This is my favourite of all soups; the ginger gives it a delicious flavour that never fails to impress. Use fresh ginger, but remember to take it out before blending.

Ingredients

500 g of carrots

1 potato

1 piece of fresh root ginger (approx. 4 cm long)

1 litre of water

2 tbsp of single cream (optional)

Salt

Pepper

Peel and chop the carrots, potato and ginger (keep the pieces of ginger large enough that you can remove them later – into quarters should do it). Place the carrots, potato and ginger in a pan and cover with the water. Bring to the boil and then simmer for 20 minutes. Remove from the heat and take out the ginger. Transfer the ingredients into a blender and blend until a smooth consistency is achieved. Season according to taste and stir in the cream if desired.

TOP TIP

Whenever a recipe tells you to simmer, make sure there are only one or two bubbles coming up every few seconds. Any more than this and you need to turn the heat down.

TOMATO SOUP

SERVES 4

Hearty and warming, this soup always makes you feel good.

Ingredients

1 kg of tomatoes

1 tbsp of olive oil

1 onion

2 tsp tomato purée

25 g of flour

500 ml of vegetable stock

1 bay leaf

Salt

Pepper

Skin the tomatoes according to the instructions in the Vegetables section (p.29). Heat the oil in a large saucepan. Peel and chop the onion and add to the pan, along with the tomatoes, purée and flour, and fry gently in the oil for about 10 minutes. Add the stock and the bay leaf, bring to the boil, then simmer for 40 minutes. Remove the bay leaf and season. Give the soup a blitz with a handheld blender if you have one, or a normal blender if you don't.

HAND BLENDER

 STUDENT GRUB

FRENCH ONION SOUP

SERVES 4

The French are passionate about their soups, and most regions have their own speciality soup which reflects the area, climate and produce. With this recipe there are no firm rules and numerous variations on the same theme occur.

Ingredients

2 large onions

1 tbsp of olive oil

2 tsp of flour

1 litre of beef or vegetable stock

Salt

Pepper

4 slices of French bread

50 g of Gruyère cheese

Peel and thinly slice the onion, then heat the oil in a saucepan and fry the onion slowly for 15 minutes, until they are a golden colour. Stir in the flour and cook for about 5 minutes, stirring the onions constantly. Add the beef or vegetable stock and bring to the boil. Season and simmer for 25 minutes. Preheat the grill. Grate the cheese onto the slices of bread. When the soup is ready pour it into a serving dish (to be authentic you should have an earthenware tureen), place the slices of bread on top of the soup and put under the grill until the cheese melts. Serve immediately.

VEGETABLE SOUP

There are no limits to what vegetables you can use – these are just a guideline.

Ingredients

2 tbsp of olive oil

1 onion

1 leek

2 cabbage leaves

1 courgette

1 carrot

1 litre of vegetable stock

1 bay leaf

Salt

Pepper

Heat the oil in a large saucepan, then peel and chop the onion and fry for about 5 minutes or until it has softened. Meanwhile, finely slice the leek, cabbage, courgette and carrot and add these to the pan. Fry for a further 10 minutes. Add the stock, bay leaf and seasoning, bring to the boil, then simmer for 30 minutes. Remove the bay leaf before serving. If you want a smoother-tasting soup then blend before serving.

PARSNIP AND APPLE SOUP

Sweet and warming – the perfect combination for a cold autumn day. A blender is required for this recipe.

Ingredients

2 tbsp of oil

1 large onion

750 g parsnips

1 apple

1 litre of vegetable stock

Salt

Pepper

Heat the oil in a large saucepan, then peel, chop and fry the onion for about 5 minutes until it has softened. Meanwhile, peel and chop the parsnips and apple, making sure you core the apple first. Add them to the pan and fry gently for a couple of minutes. Add the stock and bring to the boil, then simmer for 30 minutes. Transfer the soup into a blender and blend until smooth. Season and serve with fresh crusty bread.

SIDE DISHES

These recipes all make great accompaniments to the main dishes in the next chapter – either if you are serving a particularly hungry horde or you just want to experiment with a multitude of tastes on one plate. Some, such as the jacket potato or the cauliflower cheese, could make a light meal all of their own – just don't scrimp on the portion sizes!

JACKET POTATO

This is a traditional component of a student diet, probably due to its low cost and simplicity. It works well as an alternative to pasta or rice in many dishes or can be eaten on its own as a small meal.

Ingredients

1 potato (judge the size according to appetite)

Filling of your choice

Suggestions for fillings:

- Chilli and cheese
- Coleslaw
- Tuna and mayonnaise
- Baked beans with Worcestershire sauce and a fried egg
- Cottage cheese and chives

After stabbing your potato several times with a sharp implement (preferably a fork) to pierce the skin, bung in the oven for about 60 minutes at Gas Mark 7 (210 °C, 425 °F).

Test the potato with a skewer or a knife to see if it is cooked in the middle. For a crispier skin, drizzle a little oil and salt over the potato and wrap in silver foil before putting it in the oven. For garlic fans, an interesting alternative is to mix some finely chopped garlic with butter and dollop this inside the potato halfway through cooking, then wrap in foil to contain the juices for the remainder of the cooking time.

STUFFED PEPPERS

SERVES 4

These Italian-inspired peppers make a great alternative to a pile of soggy vegetables next to a steak or chicken breast.

Ingredients

4 peppers

2 tbsp of olive oil

1 onion

1 clove of garlic

1 tin of tomatoes

2 tsp of tomato purée

100 g of mushrooms

1 glass of red wine

1 tbsp of chopped parsley

1 tsp of chopped rosemary

2 tbsp of breadcrumbs

Salt

Pepper

Pre-heat the oven to Gas Mark 6 (200 °C, 400 °F). Cut the tops off the peppers and remove the seeds, then place in boiling water for 3 to 4 minutes. Remove and plunge in cold water.

Head the oil in a large saucepan. Peel and chop the onion and garlic, then fry for a few minutes. Add the other ingredients, bring to the boil and then simmer for 10 minutes. Fill the peppers with the mixture, replace the lid of the pepper and bake in the oven for 35 minutes.

CAULIFLOWER CHEESE

A quick and cheap dish that can be prepared with ease. Makes a great accompaniment to roast beef or pork.

Ingredients

50 g of butter

50 g of cornflour

375 ml of milk

150 g of cheese

Salt

Pepper

1 cauliflower

Prepare the cheese sauce as outlined in the Dressings, Sauces and Dips section, p.37, (using 100 g of the cheese) but use 375 ml of milk instead of 500 ml, and add seasoning. Break the cauliflower into florets then place in boiling water for about 10 minutes, making sure it is not overcooked.

When the cauliflower is cooked, drain well and place in an ovenproof dish, pour over the cheese sauce, sprinkle on the remaining 50 g of grated cheese and brown under a hot grill.

YORKSHIRE PUDDING

The perfect accompaniment to any roast (although traditionally it is only served with roast beef). The 'proper' way to cook these is to make one large pudding, but it's more common today to make lots of small ones. If you opt for the big 'un, just use the same recipe but use one large tin.

Ingredients

Pinch of salt

100 g of plain flour

1 egg

250 ml of milk

Oil

Mix the salt and flour in a mixing bowl. Beat the egg, then make a well in the flour and pour the egg in. Mix together carefully, adding the milk little by little. Beat the mixture for a few minutes until it is smooth. Pour a teaspoon of oil into individual patty tins (a bun or muffin tin would work, too), then add 2 tablespoons of the mixture into each. Bake for about 15 minutes or until they have risen and browned, but take care not to open the door of the oven whilst they are cooking (at least for the first ten minutes), or you'll end up with flat puddings!

MAIN DISHES

Main courses are the heart of cooking. The greatest moment in your culinary career may just well be when you lay down a steaming plate of delicious paella that you have made from scratch in front of all of your friends and housemates. Everything else – from starters to cakes – is a bonus, adding interest and variation, but main dishes are the place to start.

The main meals in this book have an international flavour, with the recipes being set out according to country of origin. The origins of some dishes can be unclear, however, and there are others which almost definitely did not originate in Britain, but have become British staples, wherever they stemmed from.

The mixture of recipes is diverse, ranging from the student classics like spag bol, chilli con carne and shepherd's pie to the lesser known and slightly exotic dishes such as coq au vin and Teriyaki salmon. None are too complicated, though some are unusual. Don't be put off by the title of a particular recipe – read it through first, as names can be deceptive. And don't worry if your household lacks perhaps one or two of the minor ingredients, as you can substitute most things for a similar alternative.

For those who think that any of the recipes sound a bit on the expensive side, just remember that most of them could be prepared for the cost of a few pints of beer.

BRITISH

The traditional British fare is often thought of by foreigners as comprising only fish and chips, bangers and mash, roast beef and early-morning fry-ups. However, things have changed a great deal in recent years and British gastronomy has moved on apace. Sun-dried tomatoes and truffle oil have become familiar features on many a supermarket shelf and within the 'foody's' larder. But, away from home and with a limited budget, I hope the following good old-fashioned traditional recipes will help to fill you up without breaking the bank.

COTTAGE PIE

This simple and traditional dish has stood the test of time because it is so comforting and delicious – and easy to make.

Ingredients

1 onion

1 clove of garlic

2 tbsp of olive oil

500 g of minced beef

1 tin of chopped tomatoes

1 tbsp of tomato purée

1 tsp of mixed herbs

Salt

Pepper

5 medium potatoes

Butter

Milk

Peel and chop the onion and garlic clove. Heat the oil in a largish saucepan, add the onion and garlic, and fry for 3 to 4 minutes. Add the meat and cook for another 10 minutes, then add the other ingredients, except for the potatoes, and simmer for 15 minutes.

While this is simmering, peel and boil the potatoes in a separate pan (test them with a knife – the knife should pass through the potato easily), then mash them with a knob of butter and a bit of milk. Put the meat in an ovenproof dish and cover with the potato, then put under the grill until the potato browns.

SPICY SAUSAGE CASSEROLE

SERVES 4

This is ideal for those fed up with boring old sausages and spuds. Although not a traditional British recipe, it's a sure-fire winner in my family so has earnt its place here.

Ingredients

1 onion

2 cloves of garlic

1 green pepper

2 tbsp of olive oil

2 tsp of chilli powder

1 pack of pork sausages

2 tbsp of tomato purée

250 ml of beef stock

1 tin of chopped tomatoes

1 tsp of oregano

Salt

Pepper

Peel and chop the onion and garlic cloves, and deseed and chop the pepper. Heat the oil in a largish saucepan or wok, then gently fry the onion, garlic and chilli powder for about 5 minutes. Then cut the sausages into small chunks and add to the pan, along with the pepper, and let them sizzle for about 10 minutes. Add the tomato purée, beef stock, tomatoes, oregano and seasoning and simmer for at least 15 minutes. Serve with rice and peas. Alternatively, after cooking the rice and peas add them directly to the casserole and cook for another couple of minutes.

TOAD IN THE HOLE

SERVES 4

A classic dish with a title that is about as misleading as hedgehog crisps.

Ingredients

100 g of flour

Salt

1 egg

250 ml of milk

500 g of sausages

4 tbsp of vegetable oil

Mix the flour with a pinch of salt, then make a well in the flour and break the egg into it. Add first a little milk to give a smooth texture, then pour in the rest of the milk and beat for a minute or so to form a batter. Put the sausages in a baking tin with the oil and bake for 10 minutes at Gas Mark 7 (210 °C, 425 °F). Then add the batter and cook for a further 25 minutes or until the batter has risen and is browned.

TOP TIP

Make sure you've read each recipe all the way through before you embark on its creation. You need to check you have all the right equipment, as well as ingredients, and that they are to hand, before you start.

BEEF STEW

Hearty and warming, this one will fill your kitchen with wonderful aromas that are sure to bring neighbours running. Delicious served with fresh crusty bread.

Ingredients

500 g of stewing steak

40 g of flour

Salt

Pepper

2 tbsp of olive oil

1 onion

1 clove of garlic

500 ml of beef stock

3 carrots

1 bay leaf

Cut the meat into 2.5 cm pieces and roll them in some of the flour with a little salt and pepper. Heat the oil in a casserole dish then brown the meat on all sides. Remove the meat and set aside. Peel and chop the onion and garlic and fry for 5 minutes in the casserole dish. Add the rest of the flour to the pan and fry gently. Add the stock and boil until it thickens. Peel and chop the carrots and add to the dish, and garnish with the bay leaf. Bake at Gas Mark 4 (180 °C, 350 °F) for 90 minutes, and remove the bay leaf before serving.

PORK AND CIDER CASSEROLE

SERVES 4

The origins of this recipes are unclear, but pork and apple has always been a classic culinary pairing. This version came into being as a bit of an experiment but the result is very tasty.

Ingredients

2 tbsp of olive oil

1 large onion

2 cloves of garlic

1 green pepper

4 pork chops

1 tin of chopped tomatoes

1 tbsp of tomato purée

2 tsp of mixed herbs

1 courgette

Salt

Pepper

500 ml of dry cider

1 cup of macaroni

½ cup of frozen peas

Heat the oil in a large casserole dish, then peel and chop the onion and garlic, and deseed and chop the green pepper, and fry for about 5 minutes. Then add the pork chops and fry on both sides for a couple of minutes. Add the tomatoes, purée, herbs, sliced courgette, seasoning and cider then bring to the boil.

Simmer for about 40 minutes, adding the macaroni about 10 minutes before serving and the peas about 5 minutes before. Check to see if the macaroni is cooked before serving – if it's still crunchy it needs a little longer.

COURGETTE AND BACON BAKE

SERVES 4

This very simple dish packs a flavoursome punch and can be a real comfort-food dish on a cool, drizzly autumn day (the season when courgettes are plentiful and cheap).

Ingredients

2 tbsp of olive oil

1 kg of courgettes

100 g of bacon

4 eggs

375 ml of milk

125 g of Cheddar cheese

Salt

Pepper

25 g of butter

Heat the oil in a large pan. Slice the courgettes and fry for 4 to 5 minutes, then cut the bacon into pieces and add to the pan for another couple of minutes. Beat the eggs together with the milk, add most of the grated cheese (leave some to sprinkle on top) and season. Grease a baking dish using the butter and layer the courgettes and bacon until they are used up. Pour the egg and cheese mixture over the top and sprinkle on the rest of the cheese. Bake at Gas Mark 4 (180 °C, 350 °F) for 40 minutes or until golden.

MEATBALLS

Meatballs are so versatile, and make a great accompaniment to spaghetti, rice, noodles or even mashed potato.

Ingredients

3 slices of bread (fresh or a few days old)

1 onion

1 tbsp of parsley

500 g of minced beef

1 tsp of chilli powder

1 tsp of smooth French mustard

1 egg

Salt

Pepper

2 tbsp of olive oil

Remove the crusts from the bread, then tear into minuscule pieces. Those with a blender can give them a whizz for a few seconds.

Peel and chop the onion, and chop the parsley. Mix together with the breadcrumbs and add the mince, chilli powder, mustard, beaten egg and seasoning together and mould into balls.

Heat the oil in a frying pan and fry the balls evenly for about 10 to 15 minutes, turning regularly. Don't make the balls too big or they will not cook in the middle.

LAMB AND LEEK CASSEROLE

> SERVES 4

Another hearty dish that requires minimum input but gives maximum flavour!

Ingredients

2 tbsp of olive oil

4 lamb chops

1 onion

250 g of carrots

2 leeks

Salt

Pepper

500 ml of beef/vegetable stock

100 g of peas

Heat the oil in a frying pan, then fry the chops for a couple of minutes on each side. Then peel and slice the onion and carrots and slice the leeks, and add to the pan for a few more minutes.

Transfer into a casserole dish, season, and pour the stock over. Put a lid on the dish and place in the oven at Gas Mark 4 (180 °C, 350 °F) for about 1 hour. Add the peas about 15 minutes before serving.

TUNA MORNAY

SERVES 4

This dish uses store-cupboard staples to create a satisfying dinner that will certainly impress your housemates.

Ingredients

4 eggs

1 large tin of tuna

6 tomatoes, sliced

250 ml of white sauce or cheese sauce

Salt

Pepper

25 g of cheese

Parsley or watercress

Hard boil the eggs, then cut in half, lengthways. Mix the yolks with the tuna. Slice the tomatoes and place in a greased oven dish, then place the whites of the eggs on the tomatoes.

Spoon the mixture of tuna and yolk onto the egg whites. Make the sauce according to the packet instructions or the recipe given on p.37, and pour the sauce over the mixture while it is hot. Season, then sprinkle with grated cheese.

Place in a moderate oven at Gas Mark 6 (200 °C, 400 °F) for about 20 minutes until lightly browned. Garnish with chopped parsley or watercress.

HOT CHICKEN

SERVES 4

This is the perfect dish if you love chicken but are looking for ways to spice it up a bit.

Ingredients

1 onion

1 green pepper

2 tbsp of olive oil

3 tsp of chilli powder

Salt

Pepper

4 pieces of chicken

1 tin of chopped tomatoes

Peel and chop the onion and deseed and chop the pepper. Heat the oil in a large saucepan and fry the onion for 3 to 4 minutes, then add the chilli powder, salt and pepper. Cook for another couple of minutes.

Add the chicken and the pepper and cook for about 10 minutes. Then add the tomatoes and simmer for 20–30 minutes, adding a little water if the sauce begins to burn. Serve with rice.

ROAST DINNERS

The traditional Sunday roast is still as popular as ever, and with the advent of many new and inspiring cookery shows, the options for adding your own unique twist to this classic meal are endless. Before roasting any meat you can stuff the joint with anything from the traditional stuffing (either from a packet or home-made), to fruit, herbs, spices or vegetables – or even another type of meat! Those sharing a house will find it is good to make the effort to share a roast, as it makes a pleasant change from all the rushed meals that are grabbed between lectures during the rest of the week.

Remember that when using the oven, it should be switched on 20 minutes before the joint is put in to heat it up to the correct temperature.

Roast Beef

Before throwing away the packaging for your joint, note how much it weighs. Allow 20 minutes cooking time per 500 g, plus 20 minutes on top, all at Gas Mark 7 (210 °C, 425 °F). This will allow for cooking the meat 'English style', i.e. with not too much blood seeping out. If you prefer it 'rare', cook for about 15 minutes less.

Put the joint in a roasting tin and pour 125 ml of vegetable oil over the top and the sides. Season heavily with salt and pepper and any herbs of your choice, and stick in the oven.

The joint must be 'basted' – that means spooning the oil in the tin over the top of the meat to stop it from drying out. Do this two or three times during cooking.

When the meat is cooked, carve the joint and serve with fresh vegetables and roast potatoes. Gravy can be made from the juices in the roasting tin by adding a small amount of flour and stirring over a medium heat to thicken, then bulking up with more beef stock.

Roast beef is traditionally served with Yorkshire puddings – see p.58 for a recipe.

Roast Pork

This must be cooked for a little longer than beef, as it is essential that pork is well cooked. Prepare in the same method as the beef but cook for 25 minutes per 500 g plus 25 minutes over, on the same oven setting. Baste the joint every 20 minutes. If you like garlic try sticking whole cloves in the joint before cooking.

Roast Lamb

Lamb can be quite expensive but has a wonderful flavour that makes it worth splashing out on occasionally.

Prepare in the same method as the beef and cook for 20 minutes per 500 g and 20 minutes extra on the same oven setting. Baste every 20

minutes. Add some sprigs of rosemary for extra flavour.

Roast Chicken

It is important not to overcook chicken as it loses all its flavour and is harder to carve, yet it is imperative that the meat is fully cooked through. You can check by sticking a skewer or fork into the bird, and if the juices run clear, it's good to eat.

Place the chicken in a baking tin with 125 ml of oil and season with plenty of black pepper and bake for 15 to 20 minutes per 500 g plus 20 minutes at Gas Mark 6 (200 °C, 400 °F).

ITALIAN

For those who think of Italy only as the vague backdrop to *The Merchant of Venice* laboriously studied at school, think again. You haven't lived until you have discovered the wonders of Italy and its cuisine.

Pasta is probably one of the most widely used ingredients in Italian cooking and, like the French, Italians are not hesitant in the use of garlic and fresh herbs. The advantage of cooking with pasta is that there is almost no limit to what you can do with it. Obviously there are set rules and standard recipes, but personal experimentation is important and fun.

The secret to the wonderful-tasting Italian sauces is 'reducing' it. This entails simmering the sauce until the liquid thickens and its volume reduces. When this happens the flavours are enhanced. When a recipe calls for this, allow the sauce to simmer for at least 20 minutes, stirring frequently.

BASIC TOMATO PASTA

Does what it says on the tin: simple but satisfying.

Ingredients

1 large onion

2 cloves of garlic

2 tbsp of olive oil

1 tin of chopped tomatoes

1 tbsp of tomato purée

6 fresh basil leaves or 1 tsp of dried oregano

Salt

Pepper

200 g of pasta of your choice

Peel and chop the onion and garlic. Heat the oil in a saucepan, then add the onion and garlic and fry gently for 3 to 4 minutes. When these have softened, add the tomatoes, purée, herbs, salt and pepper. Cook for another 20 minutes until they have been reduced.

Meanwhile, cook the pasta according to packet instructions and, when cooked, drain and stir together with the sauce.

To add some colour, try adding in a mixture of frozen vegetables (peas, sweetcorn, green beans) or, for a slightly more filling variation, add a glass of red wine and chopped ham to the mix before reducing.

SPAGHETTI BOLOGNESE

SERVES 4

Most students have probably tried preparing this classic Italian dish at some point. There are many variations of the recipe; this is my preferred one.

Ingredients

1 onion

2 cloves of garlic

2 tbsp of olive oil

500 g of minced beef

100 g of mushrooms

2 rashers of bacon

1 carrot

1 tin of chopped tomatoes

1 large glass of red wine (optional)

1 tbsp of tomato purée

375 ml of beef stock

Salt

Pepper

200 g of spaghetti or other pasta

Peel and chop the onion and garlic and fry gently in the oil in a large saucepan for 5 minutes, being careful not to burn them. Add the minced beef and continue frying for a further 10 minutes. Cut the mushrooms and bacon into small pieces and grate the carrot, and add these along with the other remaining ingredients.

While your sauce is reducing, which takes around 20 minutes, cook a pasta of your choice – it doesn't have to be spaghetti – according to packet instructions. It's up to you whether you want to pile the mixture on top of the pasta on a plate or combine the two, but either way a sprinkling of Parmesan on top finishes it off perfectly.

ITALIAN

CARBONARA

SERVES 3 TO 4

This version of the classic dish is a favourite in our house.

Ingredients

200 g of pasta of your choice

1 clove of garlic

6 rashers of streaky bacon

2 tbsp of olive oil

50 g of Parmesan cheese

3 egg yolks

3 tbsp single cream

Salt

Pepper

Boil the pasta in a saucepan for about 12 minutes, or according to the instructions on the packet. Five minutes before the pasta is cooked, peel and chop the garlic and cut the bacon into small pieces and fry in the oil for 4 to 5 minutes. When the pasta is cooked, drain, and add to the bacon. Then grate the cheese and beat the egg yolks, and add to the pan with the cream and seasoning. Heat until the egg has cooked, stirring constantly (this should take just a couple of minutes), then serve immediately with more black pepper.

76 STUDENT GRUB

PASTA WITH COURGETTE AND BACON SAUCE

SERVES 4

Ham works just as well in this delicious recipe if you don't have bacon.

Ingredients

1 onion

1 clove of garlic

2 tbsp of olive oil

2 courgettes

2 rashers of bacon

1 tin of chopped tomatoes

1 tbsp of tomato purée

Salt

Pepper

2 tsp of oregano

200 g of pasta of your choice

Peel and chop the onion and garlic, then fry in the oil in a large saucepan for about 3 or 4 minutes. Slice the courgettes and cut the bacon into strips and add to the pan for another 5 minutes (but don't have the heat up too high otherwise the onion will start to burn). A tablespoon of water can be added to help the cooking and to prevent any burning.

When the courgettes have softened, add the tomatoes, purée, seasoning and herbs. Simmer the sauce for at least 15 to 20 minutes. Meanwhile, cook the pasta according to the packet instructions and serve with Parmesan or grated Cheddar on top if you have any.

PARSLEY PASTA

> SERVES 2

This sounds very simple, but the taste is wonderful on its own – don't be tempted to try to make it more exciting!

Ingredients

100 g of wholemeal pasta shells

25 g of butter

25 or 50 g of Cheddar cheese

3 tbsp of fresh flat leaf parsley

Salt

Pepper

Cook the pasta according to the instructions on the packet, then drain. Add the butter and allow it to melt. Grate the cheese and roughly chop the parsley and toss in with the salt and pepper until evenly distributed, then serve immediately.

AUBERGINE BAKE

SERVES 4

Packed full of natural goodness and bursting with flavour, this is the epitome of Italian cooking.

Ingredients

1 large aubergine

2 onions

2 cloves of garlic

2 tbsp of olive oil

1 tin of tomatoes

1 tbsp of tomato purée

1 tsp of dried oregano

Salt

Pepper

125 g pot of natural yogurt

25 g of white breadcrumbs

75 g of Cheddar cheese

Prepare the veg: thinly slice the aubergine and peel and chop the onions and garlic. Heat the oil in a frying pan. Cook the aubergine in batches so that the slices aren't overlapping in the pan: fry until it has softened and slightly browned, then place on kitchen paper to absorb the oil. After cooking all the aubergine, use the same pan to fry the onion and garlic for 5 minutes.

The next stage is to add the tomato, tomato purée, oregano and seasoning to the pan. Bring to the boil, then simmer for 10 minutes before stirring in the yogurt.

Using a greased ovenproof dish, arrange the aubergine then the tomato sauce in alternate layers. Continue this until the top layer is of aubergine. Cover the top with breadcrumbs and grated cheese. Bake at Gas Mark 4 (180 °C, 350 °F), for 30 minutes.

Serve with rice or potatoes.

NUTTY RICE

This recipe is best cooked in a large wok, and is a unique (and healthy) twist on traditional rice dishes.

Ingredients

1 onion

1 clove of garlic

2 tbsp of olive oil

25 g of mushrooms

1 green pepper

1 small tin of sweetcorn

2 cups of wholemeal rice

1 vegetable stock cube

100 g of walnuts

Salt

Pepper

Fresh parsley

Peel and chop the onion and garlic, then fry in the oil in a large frying pan or wok for between 4 and 5 minutes. Chop the mushrooms and green pepper and add to the pan, along with the sweetcorn, and fry for another couple of minutes. Next add the uncooked rice and about 4 cups of water. Sprinkle the stock cube over the mixture and stir frequently. Simmer for about 20 minutes, depending on the type of rice used. Add more water if necessary to stop the rice from drying out.

If the rice is soft when pinched then it is cooked. Add the walnuts a couple of minutes before removing from the heat. Season with salt, pepper and chopped parsley.

LASAGNE

An Italian classic, loved by many, that's always a winner.

Ingredients

1 large onion

2 cloves of garlic

2 tbsp of oil

500 g of minced beef

1 tin of chopped tomatoes

2 tsp of oregano

125 ml of beef stock

2 tbsp of tomato purée

Salt

Pepper

1 packet of lasagne ('no pre-cooking required' type)

For the cheese sauce:

25 g of butter

50 g of flour

500 ml of milk

150 g of cheese

Peel and chop the onion and garlic and cook with the oil in a saucepan for 5 minutes. Add the mince and cook thoroughly. Then add the tomatoes, oregano, beef stock, tomato purée and seasoning. After bringing to the boil, an optional simmering for 15 to 20 minutes will improve the flavour.

While the meat sauce is reducing, prepare the cheese sauce. Melt the butter in a saucepan and then add the flour, stirring constantly. Remove from the heat and add the milk in stages. If the milk is added in one go, you end up with lumps in the sauce. After adding the milk, bring to the boil and add the cheese, saving a bit for the top. Then simmer for 3 or 4 minutes; the sauce should now begin to thicken.

If your sauce hasn't thickened by now, don't panic. Try adding a bit more flour, but sieve it first if you can. Lumpiness can be rectified by pouring the mixture through a sieve.

Find a shallow baking dish and grease it, then add a layer of meat sauce followed by a layer of lasagne, followed by a layer of cheese sauce. Continue this formation until you have used up your mixtures, making sure you finish with the cheese sauce. As well as sprinkling grated cheese on top, fresh tomato slices can be added.

Bake on the middle shelf of a preheated oven at Gas Mark 6 (200 °C, 400 °F) for 30 to 40 minutes.

TOP TIP

To help keep your lasagne nice and moist (none of those hard, dry edges here!) make sure you spread the sauce over every inch of the pasta, and cover the dish with foil for the first 20 minutes.

VEGETARIAN LASAGNE

SERVES 4

You can use silken tofu as a meat substitute with this recipe. It sounds like a Greek island, but it tastes a bit better than that. If you can find some, prepare in the same way as the meat lasagne, substituting the meat for tofu, reducing the cooking time slightly.

Ingredients

1 large onion

1 clove of garlic

2 tbsp of olive oil

1 leek

1 red pepper

1 green pepper

2 courgettes

1 tin of chopped tomatoes

2 tbsp of tomato purée

2 tsp of oregano

Salt

Pepper

1 packet of lasagne ('no pre-cooking required' type)

For the cheese sauce:

25 g of butter

50 g of flour

500 ml of milk

150 g of cheese

Peel and chop the onion and garlic, and cook with the oil in a large saucepan for 5 minutes. Then chop the leek, peppers and courgettes and add to the pan, frying gently for another 3 minutes or so. Then add the tomatoes, purée, oregano and seasoning, bring to the boil then simmer for a further 20 minutes. While the vegetable sauce is simmering prepare the cheese sauce.

Melt the butter in a saucepan and add the flour, stirring constantly. Remove from the heat and add the milk in stages. Then bring to the boil and add the cheese, saving a bit for the top. Simmer for 3 or 4 minutes. Add more flour if the sauce refuses to thicken.

Grease a shallow baking dish, then add a layer of vegetable sauce, a layer of lasagne, a layer of cheese sauce, a layer of lasagne, and so on, making sure to end up with cheese sauce on top. Then sprinkle on the remaining grated cheese.

Bake in a preheated oven for around 25 minutes at Gas Mark 6 (200 °C, 400 °F).

CHICKEN RISOTTO

SERVES 4

Although the chicken in this dish creates a wonderful flavour, an equally delicious version can be prepared without meat by increasing the quantity of mushrooms and replacing the stock with vegetable stock.

Ingredients

75 g of chicken

25 g of butter

1 onion

1 clove of garlic

200 g of arborio rice

500 ml of chicken stock

Salt

Pepper

50 g of mushrooms

Cut the chicken into pieces. Heat the butter in a large saucepan and fry the chicken pieces for 5 minutes, then remove from the pan and put them in a bowl.

Peel and chop the onion and garlic and fry for 3 to 4 minutes. Put the rice in a sieve and wash under cold water to remove the starch. Then add the rice to the onions and fry gently for a couple more minutes.

Prepare the stock using boiling water, then add to the rice a little at a time. Stir whilst adding the stock. Let the rice simmer gently until the stock is all absorbed and the rice is cooked. This should take about 20 minutes. Season.

When the rice is cooked, slice the mushrooms and add to the pan with the chicken and cook for a minute or so, to heat them through.

PASTA WITH SPICY SAUSAGE

> SERVES 4

It might seem like an unusual combination but it works well and it's always great to find another way of preparing the good old banger.

Ingredients

4 thick spicy sausages

350 g of tagliatelle

1 courgette

2 tbsp of olive oil

1 clove of garlic

2 tbsp of fresh basil

2 tbsp of fresh chives

2 tbsp of fresh parsley

50 g of Parmesan

25 g of butter

Salt

Pepper

Grill or fry the sausages until cooked then cut into slices. Cook the pasta according to the packet instructions with a drop of olive oil added to the water to stop it sticking together. Cut the courgette into thin strips so that they look like matchsticks and fry in a little olive oil with the peeled and crushed garlic for a couple of minutes. Finely chop the herbs and grate the cheese. When the pasta is cooked, drain and return to the pan. Throw in the cheese, herbs, sausage and butter, mix thoroughly and season. If the cheese has not melted return to the heat for a minute or two.

MACARONI CHEESE WITH TOMATO

 SERVES 4

This is another of my favourite recipes. If you don't have any macaroni try using other pasta shapes such as shells, twists or quills.

Ingredients

25 g of butter

25 g of flour or cornflour

375 ml of milk

150 g of Cheddar cheese

100 g of macaroni

2 large tomatoes

Salt

Pepper

Melt the butter in a saucepan and mix in the flour, then gradually add the milk, stirring constantly to avoid lumps. Bring to the boil, add the grated cheese (leave a little aside for the topping), then leave to simmer for 3 to 4 minutes.

Now cook the macaroni or pasta according to the instructions on the packet. When this is done, drain and mix with the cheese sauce. Put into a baking dish, top with sliced tomatoes and the rest of the cheese, season, and then grill until browned.

ITALIAN

POTATO AND TOMATO CAKE

> **SERVES 4**

These little cakes are easy to make, cheap and wholesome – a great, comforting dinner or perfect as a snack when cold.

Ingredients

1 onion

2 tbsp of olive oil

1 tin of chopped tomatoes

Salt

Pepper

1 kg of 'old' potatoes

Peel and chop the onion, then fry gently in the oil for 10 minutes. Add the tomatoes, salt and pepper. Keep the heat low and simmer for about 20 minutes so the sauce reduces to a thick liquid.

Whilst the sauce is reducing, boil the potatoes until they are soft enough to mash. This will take between 15 and 20 minutes, and you can tell they are done by poking a fork through them – if it goes through easily, they are ready to mash. Gradually mix the sauce with the mashed potatoes.

When all the sauce is added, spoon the mixture out onto a serving plate and mould into the shape of a cake. If you like the edges crispy, you can fry them in a little oil for a few minutes on each side until lightly browned. Eat hot or cold.

PIZZA

Ah pizza, a sacred food amongst students. The takeaway option may be tempting, but making your own is fun and easy. There is huge scope for variety here, both in toppings and bases, so don't be afraid to experiment! The easiest to make is the French bread pizza, because the base is simply a sliced baguette. Dough bases can be bought ready-made, but they cost more than French sticks or home-made doughs.

Pizza Margherita

SERVES 1

This is the basic pizza. If you want to design your own, use this and add your own toppings. To add a touch of authenticity, sprinkle some basil on top – the mozzarella, tomato and basil recreate the colours of the Italian flag.

Ingredients

1 stick of French bread

2 tbsp tomato purée

50 g of mozzarella cheese

Pepper

Pinch of oregano

1 tsp of olive oil

Slice the French stick in half and spread some tomato purée on top. A thin layer will do – if you put too much on your pizza it will become soggy. Place slices of the cheese on top, season, add the oregano (and basil if desired) and pour on the oil. Bake in the oven until the cheese turns a golden brown colour. It should take roughly 15 minutes at Gas Mark 7 (210 °C, 425 °F). If you don't like/can't afford mozzarella, ordinary Cheddar cheese does the trick, but is slightly less Italian!

Pizza Roma

 SERVES 1

The tuna and onion create a wonderful a-Roma in this Italian classic!

Ingredients

1 stick of French bread

2 tbsp tomato purée

50 g of tuna

2 to 3 onion rings

25 g of cheese

Pepper

Pinch of oregano

1 tsp of oil

Slice the French stick in half and spread some tomato purée on top. Scatter the tuna on top first, then the onion rings and finally the grated cheese. Season, add the oregano and oil and cook as for the previous recipe.

Other variations:

There is almost no limit to what you can put on a pizza. Here is a list of suggested toppings that can be used as a basis for designing your own.

- Anchovies
- Capers
- Egg
- Exotic cheeses
- Fresh tomatoes
- Green peppers
- Ham
- Hot green chilli peppers
- Leeks

- Mushrooms
- Olives
- Onions
- Pepperoni
- Pineapple
- Red peppers
- Spinach
- Sultanas
- Sweetcorn
- Tuna

FRENCH

The French like to think of themselves as producing the best lovers, the finest wines, and exquisitely smelly cheeses. Perhaps, though, the thing they excel at the most is producing delicious and palette-tingling dishes fit for royalty – food which tastes extremely good when washed down with a few litres of Beaujolais.

MOULES MARINIÈRES

SERVES 4

This may sound a little luxurious when you're cooking on a budget but mussels can be surprisingly good value, and should be available at the fish counter of your local supermarket.

Ingredients

2 kg of mussels

2 cloves of garlic

4 shallots

25 g of butter

1 tsp olive oil

400 ml of dry white wine

2 tbsp of parsley

Salt

Pepper

Scrub the mussels and remove the 'beards' that are usually attached to them (the little tufts that hang out the end) by pulling them towards the hinge of the mussel. If there are any mussels that are already open or cracked discard them. Soak them in cool water for 20 minutes to encourage them to 'spit' out any sand. Meanwhile, peel and finely chop the garlic and shallots. Heat the butter and oil in a large saucepan and gently cook the shallots and garlic with the wine and chopped parsley for 5 minutes. Add the mussels, turn up the heat and cook for about 5 minutes. Whilst the mussels are cooking shake the pan a couple of times. This helps the mussels to open and ensures they are cooked evenly.

When cooked, remove any mussels that have not opened. Reduce the juices left in the pan by boiling rapidly for a few minutes. The mussels should be served immediately with seasoning and a little chopped parsley on top.

COQ AU VIN

SERVES 4

This legendary recipe is perfect on a cold winter's evening. It is traditionally made using red wine from the Burgundy region of France. Burgundy produces some of the finest wines in the world, but they come at a price, usually a high one. If you are on a budget use a robust wine from a cheaper region. It doesn't really matter where you get your coq from.

Ingredients

50 g of butter

1 kg of chicken thighs or drumsticks

10 shallots

1 clove of garlic

225 g of small mushrooms

100 g of streaky bacon

3 tbsp of brandy (optional)

300 ml of red wine

150 ml of chicken stock

1 bay leaf

Salt

Pepper

1 tbsp of fresh parsley

For the *beurre manié*:

2 tbsp flour

2 tbsp butter

Melt the butter in a large casserole dish, then fry the chicken pieces for 5 minutes. Remove from the dish and set aside. Peel and chop the shallots and garlic, chop the mushrooms and cut the bacon into strips, then fry for 5 minutes. Now add the chicken pieces. If you are using it, pour brandy over the chicken and set alight (a miniature brandy bottle could be purchased for this dish to keep the budget down). Once the alcohol has burned itself out (i.e. when the flame dies) pour in the red wine and stock, and add the bay leaf and seasoning, then bring to the boil. Simmer for about 2 hours. Whilst the chicken is simmering prepare what is known as the *beurre manié* by mixing the flour and the butter together to form a soft paste. Split the *beurre manié* into small pieces and drop into the sauce in your casserole dish, stirring constantly. Remove the bay leaf before serving and garnish with the chopped parsley.

Make sure to taste as you go, adjusting flavourings as necessary.

CHICKEN IN BEER

The temptation is always to leave out the chicken from this recipe, but aim for restraint.

Ingredients

1 onion

2 tbsp of olive oil

4 chicken pieces

3 carrots

1 leek

100 g of mushrooms

1 large can of your favourite lager/ale

Salt

Pepper

Peel and chop the onion, then fry in the oil in a casserole dish for 3 to 4 minutes. Add the chicken and fry for another 10 minutes. Slice the carrots, leek and mushrooms and chuck them in the dish along with the lager/ale and seasoning, then stick in the oven for 1 hour at Gas Mark 5 (190 °C, 375 °F).

Then finish off the four-pack of beer, taking care not to get so drunk that you forget to take the chicken out of the oven.

FRENCH

PORK PROVENÇAL

> SERVES 4

This recipe is based on one of the fine offerings of Hotel du Commerce, Castellane.

Ingredients

1 onion

1 clove of garlic

2 tbsp of olive oil

1 tin of chopped tomatoes

1 red pepper

1 courgette

2 tsp of herbes de Provence or mixed herbs

Salt

Pepper

4 pork chops

4 slices of Cheddar cheese

Peel and chop the onion and garlic, then fry in the oil in a saucepan for about 5 minutes. When these have cooked, add the tomatoes, chopped red pepper and courgette, herbs and seasoning. Let the sauce simmer for 20 minutes. After 10 minutes, grill the pork on foil, turning occasionally, and when it is nearly cooked put some sauce and the slices of cheese on the pork and grill until the cheese begins to melt.

Note that thinner pork chops will take less cooking time.

Serve with potatoes and fresh vegetables and the rest of the sauce.

LEMON CHICKEN

SERVES 2

A refreshing and zesty twist on a simple chicken dish.

Ingredients

2 chicken breasts

2 tbsp of olive oil

Juice of 1 lemon

Salt

Pepper

Cut the chicken into small pieces (this allows the lemon to flavour a larger area). Heat the oil in large frying pan then add the chicken, lemon juice and seasoning. Fry for 5 minutes, or until the chicken is cooked all the way through, adding more lemon juice before serving if required.

Serve with a salad and pitta or French bread.

TOP TIP

Let your pan heat up fully before adding the oil and the ingredients – if you follow the timings of recipes starting with a cold pan, you may undercook it.

RATATOUILLE

> SERVES 4

This traditional Provençal recipe can really be made from whatever vegetables are available. Tinned tomatoes are cheaper than buying fresh ones (except in the summer when fresh ones are more affordable) and they often taste better, too. The lemon is considered optional by some, but I believe it to be essential.

Ingredients

1 small aubergine

2 onions

2 cloves of garlic

1 courgette

1 lemon (optional)

1 red pepper

2 tbsp of olive oil

1 tin of chopped tomatoes

2 tsp of rosemary

1 bay leaf

1 glass of red wine, water or tomato juice (optional)

Salt

Pepper

Before you prepare the other vegetables, place the pieces of aubergine on a plate and sprinkle them with salt. Then peel and finely chop the onion and garlic, thinly slice the courgette, quarter the lemon and deseed and chop the red pepper. Now wash the aubergine pieces to remove the salt then dry them with kitchen paper, and dice. Heat the oil in a large saucepan. Fry the onions and garlic for about 5 minutes, then add the courgette, the aubergine and the pepper. Cook for about 5 minutes then add the tomatoes, lemon and other ingredients. Bring to the boil and then simmer for 20 minutes.

Ratatouille can be served with almost anything – rice, baked potato, pitta bread, etc. It can also be served cold.

QUICHE

Once the basic technique of making a quiche is mastered, limitless combinations of this classic French dish can be produced. Many people are put off preparing a quiche because it involves making pastry, but it is not as hard as it sounds (and if you really cannot face making it yourself packs of the stuff are readily available in most supermarkets).

For this recipe a 20 cm flan dish and a rolling pin are needed.

Shortcrust Pastry Crust

Ingredients

200 g of plain flour

Pinch of salt

100 g of butter

3 tbsp of water

This is perhaps one of the only times when I would make the effort to sieve the flour and salt, but don't worry if you don't possess such an implement. After sieving the flour and the salt add the butter. It is easier to rub in if the butter is cut into little cubes.

The term 'rubbing in' is the procedure in which, using the fingertips, the flour and the fat are combined to produce a mixture the consistency of fine breadcrumbs. It's best if you have cool hands to make this job easier.

After rubbing in, add some water a little at a time. The water is needed to bind the mixture together, but be careful not to add so much as to make the pastry become sticky. Mould the pastry into a ball then roll out on a floured board or very clean floured work surface. Also sprinkle a coating of flour onto the rolling pin (you can always improvise with a wine bottle if you don't have a rolling pin). The flour is used to stop the pastry from sticking to the board and the pin.

Roll the pastry so that its area is big enough to cover the flan dish, then carefully place the pastry over the dish and mould it in the shape of the dish. Remove the edge of the overlapping pastry by running a knife along the rim of dish.

The next stage is to make the filling of the quiche.

Cheese and Onion Quiche

A simple yet delicious quiche filling, and one that you will probably be able to prepare using bits from your fridge without having to buy in special ingredients.

Ingredients for filling

1 onion

1 tbsp of olive oil

4 eggs

250 ml of milk

Salt

Pepper

100 g of Cheddar cheese

Peel and chop the onion, then fry in the oil in a frying pan for a couple of minutes. Place the onion on the bottom of the pastry case. Beat the eggs together, add the milk, season and beat again. Pour this over the onion, grate the cheese and sprinkle on top, then bake in a hot oven at Gas Mark 6 (200 °C, 400 °F) for 25 minutes or until the filling is cooked (it should be springy to the touch at the centre of the quiche – if it's still liquid it will need a little longer in the oven).

Quiche Lorraine

SERVES 4

The most famous quiche of all has to be the Lorraine. Its name derives from its region of origin, and it is delicious eaten hot or cold. Unfortunately I have had to corrupt this recipe slightly by cutting out the cream as this makes it rather expensive for students. But if you are feeling flush then half the milk can be substituted for single cream: it's well worth it.

Ingredients for filling

100 g of bacon

4 eggs

250 ml of milk

Salt

Pepper

50 g of cheese (optional)

Cut the bacon into small pieces, then fry lightly for a couple of minutes and place on the bottom of the pastry base. Beat the eggs together, add the milk, season and beat again.

Pour over the bacon, grate the cheese and sprinkle on top if desired and bake in a hot oven at Gas Mark 6 (200 °C, 400 °F) for 25 minutes or until the filling has set.

ORIENTAL

With the availability of fresh oriental produce in most supermarkets, many people have taken to home experimentation, rather than forking out for a takeaway. Oriental food is rich in flavours, giving you a chance to experiment with some delicious vegetables and spices which aren't quite so common in western food; think ginger, coconut milk, pak choi, water chestnuts and soy sauce. In most of these recipes the meat can be replaced with tofu for an authentic and veggie-friendly alternative.

FISH WITH GINGER

SERVES 1 TO 2

Ginger is a quintessential ingredient in eastern cuisine, and for good reason – it's utterly delicious!

Ingredients

1 whole fish, cleaned (bass or rock work well, or a 300 g cod fillet)

1 clove of garlic

25 g of fresh ginger

Juice of 1 lime

2 tsp of soy sauce

Place the fish on a piece of tin foil. Peel the garlic and ginger, chopping the garlic finely and thinly slicing the ginger. Mix the lime juice, soy sauce, garlic and ginger together and pour over the fish. Seal the fish up in the foil and bake in the oven for 40 minutes at Gas Mark 5 (190 °C, 375 °F). Serve with a selection of vegetables such as spring onions and mangetout.

THAI FISH CAKES

SERVES 3

This is a jazzed-up version of the fish cakes your mum used to make – always a sure-fire winner.

Ingredients

4 spring onions

2 tbsp of fresh coriander

500 g of white fish, such as cod or haddock

2 tsp of Thai red curry paste

1 tsp of fish sauce

1 tsp of lime juice

Salt

Pepper

2 tbsp of vegetable oil

Chop the spring onions and fresh coriander, then place all the ingredients into a food processor, except the oil, and give a quick blitz. Don't overdo it or it will end up being a purée. Remove the mixture and shape into small patties. You should be able to make about 12 small fish cakes.

Heat the oil in a frying pan and fry the fish cakes in batches until golden brown.

Serve with a herb salad and Thai dipping sauce.

TERIYAKI SALMON

SERVES 2

The taste of salmon alone is enough to make most people drool, but add teriyaki and ginger and you get a gloriously tasty dish every time.

Ingredients

3 tsp of fresh ginger

4 tbsp of teriyaki sauce

1 tsp of sugar

1 tbsp of water

1 tsp of sesame oil

2 salmon fillets

To create the marinade, peel and grate the ginger, then combine with the teriyaki sauce, sugar, water and oil in a bowl big enough to hold the salmon fillets. Place the salmon fillets in the marinade and leave for 30 minutes.

Remove the salmon from the marinade and place on tin foil and grill for approximately 10 minutes depending on the thickness of the fillet.

Delicious served with steamed pak choi.

RED THAI CURRY

The intense flavours of this dish have made it a classic the world over. If you're feeling adventurous you could try varying the amount of curry paste to suit your palette (the more you use, the spicier it gets!) or even adding extra ingredients such as prawns, green beans, onion or red peppers.

Ingredients

1 tbsp of groundnut oil

1 tbsp of red Thai curry paste

3 chicken breasts

1 400 ml tin of coconut milk

1 cup of water

1 red pepper

2 tsp of brown sugar

2 tsp of grated lime rind

1 tbsp of fish sauce

Heat the oil in a wok or large frying pan. Add the curry paste and cook for a minute, stirring as it cooks. Don't let it burn.

Cut the chicken into chunks and stir-fry for 3 to 4 minutes, after which add the coconut milk and water. Bring to the boil, then chop and deseed the red pepper and add to the wok, then simmer for 10 minutes. Finally, add the sugar, lime and fish sauce and cook gently for a further 5 minutes.

Serve with rice.

STIR-FRY

Those fortunate enough to possess a wok will find oriental cooking a lot easier than those stuck with the indignity of a frying pan. If you do have to use a frying pan use the biggest one you have. The wok is one of my most-used kitchen accessories – its use does not have to be confined to oriental cooking alone.

It is up to you what to put in a stir-fry, though it is often a good way of using up any spare vegetables that are lurking in the back of your cupboard before they undergo a metamorphosis into a different life form.

Vegetable Stir-fry

SERVES 2

Your basic stir-fry – healthy, tasty and surprisingly filling.

Ingredients

1 onion

1 clove of garlic

1 carrot

1 red pepper

1 green pepper

2 tbsp of olive oil

1 tin of water chestnuts

1 tin of bamboo shoots

2 tbsp of soy sauce

Salt

Pepper

1 pack of fresh beansprouts

Prepare all the vegetables first: peel and chop the onion, garlic and carrot, and chop and deseed the red and green peppers. Pour the oil into your wok or frying pan over a high heat, then when it is smoking (try not to set fire to the kitchen in the process), add the onion and garlic, and fry for 5 minutes, stirring constantly. If you are using water chestnuts, cook these first as they take the longest to cook, and are nicer when they are slightly crispy. Then add the soy sauce, seasoning and other vegetables except for the beansprouts.

After frying the vegetables for about 5 to 10 minutes, add the beansprouts and cook for a couple more minutes. It is important to keep the beansprouts firm.

Serve with rice or noodles.

Pork Stir-fry

SERVES 2

The pork really lifts the flavour of this dish, but you could try using other meats too – just make sure they're cooked right through.

Ingredients

1 onion

1 clove of garlic

1 green pepper

2 tbsp of olive oil

1 tbsp of soy sauce

2 tsp of chilli powder

250 g of diced pork

Peel and chop the onion and garlic, and chop and deseed the pepper. Heat the oil in a large frying pan or wok, then fry the onion and the garlic for about 3 to 4 minutes. Add the pepper, soy sauce, chilli powder and the pork and fry until the pork is cooked. This should take about 10 minutes, depending on the size of the meat pieces. Serve with rice.

COCONUT AND CHICKEN SOUP

SERVES 4

This recipe is based on a dish that I had in a restaurant on a remote island in Thailand. I had some of the best meals in my life in MaMa's, even though the restaurant was hardly more than a tin shack.

Ingredients

3 chicken breasts

2 tbsp of olive oil

50 g of fresh ginger

Pinch of curry powder

1 tsp of flour

Salt

Pepper

75 g of soluble coconut

4 tbsp of cream (optional)

Remove the skin from the chicken, then chop into bite-sized pieces. Heat the oil in a large saucepan, and fry the chicken for about 5 minutes, turning frequently to stop it sticking to the pan.

Using a sharp knife remove the outer layer of the ginger and then slice it into thin pieces. Don't make the pieces too small as they shouldn't be eaten. Add the ginger, curry powder, flour and seasoning to the chicken.

Dissolve the coconut in water – it is easier if the water is hot. Add the coconut to the other ingredients, bring to the boil, then simmer for 15 to 20 minutes. The cream should be added 5 minutes before serving.

Serve the soup with a side order of rice.

INDIAN

Curry is one dish that most students are familiar with, though not always when in a state of complete consciousness. Some of the best evenings result from staying in to watch a DVD with a four-pack and a vindaloo, or a bottle of wine and a tandoori chicken.

What a lot of students miss out on is the joy of making your own version of the classics. Half an hour in the kitchen could yield a curry that would last you and your mates a few days and still be cheaper than buying from the local Taj. It is unfortunate that some people seem to just try to produce the hottest curry they can by shovelling in a tin of curry powder and a dozen chillies, so they can impress their friends with their machismo. The idea of curry is to produce a combination of flavours and tastes that harmonise together, not to produce a vile discord and numb your mouth into oblivion.

Indian cooking for most people is simplified by using ready-prepared curry powders. This, although it will undoubtedly produce a curry, will not represent the true flavour of India. Purists will know that the secret of Indian gastronomy is in the use of a vast combination of different spices and flavourings. I am not saying you can't make a good curry without these spices, but they certainly make a difference to the taste.

If you share my passion for Indian food it is worthwhile reading some specialist cookbooks. They will explain about the wide variety of spices available, and will give you an authentic taste of Indian cuisine.

VEGETABLE CURRY

There are literally thousands of different recipes for curry, but a vegetable curry is both amazingly cheap and as suited for freezing as the South Pole. So why not make a bit extra and save it for when the money runs out mid-term?

Ingredients

1 onion

2 cloves of garlic

2 tbsp of olive oil

1 tbsp of Madras curry powder

4 potatoes

2 courgettes

1 leek

1 tin of chopped tomatoes

1 dried red chilli

250 ml of vegetable stock

Any spare vegetables

1 to 2 tbsp of water

Salt

Pepper

1 small pot of natural yogurt

Peel and chop the onion and garlic, then fry in the oil in a large saucepan with the curry powder for 5 minutes or until the onion has softened. Dice the potatoes into 2.5 cm cubes, and slice the courgettes and leek. Add these to the pan, along with all the other ingredients except the yogurt. Season, then bring to the boil, and simmer for 40 minutes or more. Add the yogurt 5 minutes before serving.

Whilst the curry is simmering taste it to see if it is to the strength required. If it is not hot enough for your asbestos-lined mouth just add more curry powder. Serve with rice – use basmati rice if you can for the best flavour, though any long-grain rice will be fine.

CHICKEN CURRY

You can't go wrong with this absolute classic.

Ingredients

2 onions

2 cloves of garlic

2 tbsp of olive oil

3 tsp of curry powder

1 tsp of garam masala

2 fresh green chilli peppers

4 chicken pieces

1 to 2 tbsp of water

Salt

Pepper

1 tin of chopped tomatoes

3 whole green cardamom pods

2 tbsp of coriander

1 small pot of natural yogurt

Peel and chop the onions and garlic and fry in the oil in a large saucepan for 5 minutes or until they have softened.

Add the curry powder, garam masala and chillies, chopped into rings, and fry for a couple more minutes. Add the chicken and water and fry for 5 minutes. Season. Add the chopped tomatoes, cardamom pods and chopped coriander. About 5 minutes before serving, add the yogurt. Simmer for 30 to 40 minutes, then serve with rice.

CURRIED EGGS

 SERVES 4

It may sound like an odd combination, but it's a simple and delicious dish which proved to be a real favourite in Victorian times.

Ingredients

4 eggs

1 onion

25 g of butter

3 tsp of curry powder

4 tomatoes

2 tsp of tomato purée

Salt

Pepper

125 ml of water

1 small pot of natural yogurt

Place the eggs in a saucepan with some water and boil for 8 minutes. While the eggs are boiling, peel and chop the onion and fry in the butter in a frying pan with the curry powder for 5 minutes. Then stir in the tomatoes (finely chopped), tomato purée, salt, pepper and the water. Bring to the boil, then simmer for 10 to 15 minutes. Peel the eggs then cut them in half and add them to the curry with the yogurt. Simmer for another 5 minutes then serve with rice.

TOP TIP

Plunge eggs into cold water after cooking to prevent the yolks from turning grey.

CHICKEN TANDOORI

> SERVES 4

Making your own tandoori will cost much less than buying from a takeaway or even a supermarket. This dish is delicious eaten cold with salad.

Ingredients

4 chicken pieces (breast, thigh or wing)

1 clove of garlic

1 tbsp of tandoori powder

250 ml of plain unsweetened natural yogurt

Remove the skin from the chicken and make some small incisions in the flesh with a sharp knife – this is to allow the marinade to penetrate deep into the chicken.

Peel and finely chop the garlic, then mix with the tandoori powder and yogurt and rub some of the mixture into the incisions of the chicken. Leave to marinate for at least 3 hours, turning occasionally. The longer it is left the more flavour it will gain.

Place the chicken in a dish and spoon over some more marinade. Cook under a medium-heat grill for about 20 minutes. Turn the chicken over every few minutes to prevent burning. Serve hot or cold.

LENTIL CURRY

The lentils give this dish a delicious texture, and you can make it as hot or mild as you like – just alter the amount of curry powder you use.

Ingredients

100 g of lentils

2 tbsp of olive oil

4 carrots

1 onion

1 courgette

1 leek

2 fresh tomatoes

1 tbsp of curry powder

Salt

Pepper

250 ml of vegetable stock

Soak the lentils in cold water for 1 hour (unless they are the kind that specify 'no soaking required'). Boil them for about 7 minutes and drain. Peel and chop the carrots and onion and slice the courgette, leek and tomatoes. Heat the oil in a large saucepan, then fry the onions and curry powder for 5 minutes. Add the other vegetables, season and fry for another 5 minutes. Add the stock and lentils, bring to the boil, then simmer for 1 hour, stirring frequently. Serve with rice.

GREEK, TURKISH AND HUNGARIAN

Greek or Turkish food should always conjure up images of luscious beaches, rocky islands and clean, blue seas. As students, however, kebabs might be more reminiscent of a night's heavy drinking. Hungary, while not necessarily famed for its food, has provided us with two of my favourite recipes in this whole book; definitely not to be missed, and they go down well with a bottle of Hungarian 'Bull's Blood' – a very dark and full-bodied red wine. Whether you eat this food sober, drunk or hungover, it's bound to taste great!

SHISH KEBAB

This dish originated in Turkey, where the first kebabs consisted of a vertically stacked pile of meat. The shish kebab as we know it today is a staple of the British takeaway scene, but homemade tastes so much better and is often far healthier.

Ingredients

375 g of lamb

1 pot of natural yogurt

Juice of 1 lemon

1 tbsp of olive oil

Salt

Pepper

Fresh rosemary

Prepare this meal well in advance, as the lamb has to marinate for at least a couple of hours in order to obtain its full flavour. Cut the lamb into small cubes and place in a bowl with the yogurt, lemon juice, olive oil and seasoning. Stir well, then put the bowl in the fridge for a couple of hours, making sure the lamb is evenly coated in the marinade.

When ready to be cooked, soak 4 wooden skewers in water for a few minutes, then divide the meat onto them, place on the grill pan with the rosemary and grill for 10 to 15 minutes, turning the kebabs occasionally so they cook evenly. If there is any spare marinade use it to flavour the meat while it is being grilled.

Serve with salad and pitta bread.

VEGETABLE KEBABS

> SERVES 2

Grilling the vegetables helps them retain their nutrients, as well as their flavour: a healthy and delicious dish – what more could you ask for?

Ingredients

1 small onion

1 pepper

1 courgette

2 tomatoes

4 mushrooms

25 g of butter

Salt

Pepper

Soak a couple of wooden skewers in water for a few minutes. Meanwhile, peel the onion and deseed the pepper, then cut all the vegetables into large chunks, or quarters. Thread all the vegetables onto them and daub them with butter. Place under a medium grill for about 15 minutes. For a different flavour try adding a tablespoon of runny honey or a dash of soy sauce whilst grilling or barbecuing. Season and serve with rice.

TOP TIP

The majority of the nutrients in fruit and vegetables are retained in the skin. If possible, always scrub vegetables clean rather than peeling away their precious skins!

MOUSSAKA

SERVES 4

This is the Greek equivalent to shepherd's pie – a warm and comforting hug of a dish.

Ingredients

1 large aubergine
2 tbsp of olive oil
2 onions
1 clove of garlic
500 g of minced beef or lamb
Salt
Pepper
1 tin of chopped tomatoes
1 tbsp of tomato purée
25 g of butter
25 g of flour
375 ml of milk
100 g of cheese

Slice the aubergine and fry with a tablespoon of oil in a frying pan until it is soft. Then place on a piece of kitchen towel to absorb the fat. Peel and chop the onions and garlic. Put some more oil in the frying pan if needed and fry the onions, garlic and meat. After about 10 minutes, season and add the tomatoes and purée.

Grease a casserole dish with either butter or oil, and fill it with alternate layers of aubergine and meat, finishing with a layer of aubergine.

To make the cheese sauce, melt the butter in a saucepan, add the flour, and mix together. Remove from the heat, and very gradually add the milk. Boil until the sauce thickens, then remove from the heat and grate in 75 g of the cheese. Pour the cheese sauce over the top of the aubergine, and sprinkle on the rest of the grated cheese. Bake for 40 minutes at Gas Mark 5 (190 °C, 375 °F).

GOULASH

This Hungarian dish traditionally uses veal, but beef makes a very good substitute too.

Ingredients

1 large onion

1 clove of garlic

2 tbsp of olive oil

500 g of stewing beef

1 red pepper

1 green pepper

1 tin of chopped tomatoes

1 tbsp of paprika

½ tsp of caraway seeds

1 tsp of mixed herbs

Salt

Pepper

375 ml of beef stock

500 g of potatoes

100 g of mushrooms

125 ml of soured cream (optional)

Peel and chop the onion and garlic and fry with the oil for a couple of minutes in a casserole dish or a large saucepan. Cut the meat into cubes and deseed and chop the peppers. Add these to the dish along with the tomatoes, paprika, caraway seeds, herbs, salt and pepper, and cook for about 5 minutes.

Add the stock to the pan and simmer for about 40 minutes. Peel and slice the potatoes and add them, and cook for another 30 minutes, then slice and add the mushrooms. Simmer for a further 10 minutes, then add the soured cream, if desired.

Serve with bread dumplings, buttered bread or salad.

CHICKEN PAPRIKA

This hearty dish is full of punchy flavour without the spicy heat of a curry and is an excellent alternative if you are not keen on Indian cuisine.

Ingredients

2 large onions

1 clove of garlic

2 tbsp of olive oil

4 chicken thighs

1 tbsp of paprika

Salt

Pepper

125 ml of chicken stock

125 ml of soured cream

Peel and finely chop the onions and garlic and fry gently in the oil in a casserole dish for about 5 minutes. Skin the chicken and add to the dish with the paprika and continue to fry for a few minutes. Season, add the stock, and simmer for 30 minutes.

Just before serving, stir in the soured cream. Serve with rice or potatoes.

MEXICAN

The atmospheric temperature of Mexico is reflected in the food (it's damn hot), so go easy with the chilli unless you're sure everyone at the table can take the heat!

CHILLI CON CARNE

This tends to go down with students almost as well as a pint of beer. The chilli can be made as hot as required, but remember that even though you may love to sweat, your housemates might prefer it a little milder.

Ingredients

1 large onion

2 cloves of garlic

2 tbsp of olive oil

3 tsp of chilli powder

500 g of minced beef

1 or 2 red/green chilli peppers

1 tin of chopped tomatoes

1 tsp of oregano

1 tbsp of tomato purée

Salt

Pepper

125 ml of beef stock

1 glass of red wine (optional)

1 tin of kidney beans

Peel and finely chop the onion and garlic, and fry in the oil with the chilli powder for about 5 minutes. Add the mince, and cook for about 10 minutes, stirring constantly to stop it burning. Add the other ingredients, except the kidney beans, varying the amounts of seasoning according to taste. Bring to the boil then simmer for about 20 minutes (the longer the better). Drain the kidney beans and add them to the pan 5 minutes before serving.

Serve with rice, pitta bread or jacket potatoes.

NACHOS

This is a great dish for sharing with friends, and you don't even need cutlery.

Ingredients

1 large onion

2 cloves of garlic

2 tbsp of olive oil

1 green pepper

2 tsp of chilli powder

1 tin of chopped tomatoes

1 tbsp of tomato purée

Salt

Pepper

1 large bag of tortilla chips

100 g of cheese

Peel and finely chop the onion and garlic, then fry in the oil in a large saucepan for 3 to 4 minutes. Chop and deseed the green pepper and add to the pan, along with the chilli powder, and cook for another couple of minutes. Then add the tomatoes, tomato purée and seasoning and cook for about 15 minutes.

Whilst the sauce is cooking, arrange the tortilla chips in a ceramic dish. When the sauce is ready, pour over the chips and finally cover with grated cheese. Then place under a hot grill until the cheese has melted, and serve with guacamole or sour cream.

SPANISH

If your diet has room to become a little more adventurous than usual, there are plenty of delicious Spanish dishes such as fabada, cocido and, of course, paella, which can be washed down with copious quantities of sangria.

PAELLA

This is probably Spain's most well-known dish. It traditionally uses seafood like prawns and mussels, but these can be left out if they are over your budget. To make this dish suitable for vegetarians, just replace the seafood and chicken with plenty of extra veggies, and remember to swap the chicken stock for vegetable.

Ingredients

2 onions

2 cloves of garlic

4 tbsp of olive oil

Salt

Pepper

200 g of rice

4 tomatoes

Pinch of saffron

500 ml of chicken stock

4 chicken pieces

1 green pepper

100 g of frozen peas

100 g of cooked mussels (optional)

100 g of peeled prawns (optional)

Peel and chop the onions and garlic, and fry in half of the oil in a large frying pan, or preferably a wok, for 3 to 4 minutes. Season. Remove the seeds from the tomatoes (cut in half from side to side – not top to bottom – and squeeze gently until the seeds have all come out). Add the rice, saffron, tomatoes and stock, bring to the boil, then cook gently for 10 minutes.

Fry the chicken in a separate pan with the remaining oil for 10 minutes or until lightly browned. Then add the chicken to the rice, deseed and chop the green pepper and stir in along with all of the other ingredients, and simmer until the rice is cooked (this can take up to another 30 minutes, but keep tasting the rice throughout cooking to check). Serve with lemon wedges.

SPANISH OMELETTE

There are numerous variations on this meal, so feel free to let your creative juices run wild. Try adding spinach, peppers, olives or even chorizo.

Ingredients

1 potato

4 eggs

1 onion

2 tomatoes

25 g of peas

Mixed herbs

Salt

Pepper

Chop the potato into small cubes, then boil for 10 minutes. Beat the eggs in a bowl and season. Peel and chop the onion and slice the tomatoes, then add to the bowl with the potato, peas, herbs and seasoning. Mix together, then pour into a flan dish. Bake at Gas Mark 6 (200 °C, 400 °F) for 15 to 20 minutes or until the mixture ceases to be runny.

Serve with a green salad and a pair of maracas.

PIPERADE

This is one of those dishes that is quick and easy to prepare and is suitable for a light lunch or supper. The dish originates from the Basque country. Add a pinch of paprika if you want it with a little bite, or ham if you want to bulk it up.

Ingredients

2 red peppers

2 green peppers

6 tomatoes

2 cloves of garlic

1 tbsp of fresh basil

2 tbsp of butter

Salt

Pepper

6 eggs

Cut the peppers into strips and deseed them, and skin and chop the tomatoes (you could use tinned tomatoes, although it won't have the same consistency). Peel and chop the garlic, and chop the basil. Heat the butter in a frying pan and cook the peppers for 10 minutes. Add the tomatoes, garlic, basil and seasoning and cook until the tomatoes are almost a pulp. Take care that the vegetables do not burn. Whilst the vegetables are cooking, beat the eggs in a basin. When the vegetables are ready add the eggs. Stir the mixture until it thickens, but do not let the eggs set completely.

AMERICAN

The Land of Plenty has many culinary delights to offer. America is well-known for its classic variations of European dishes, such as hot dogs, burgers and the humble pizza, but they have some fantastic original dishes too. Here are just a few of my favourites.

BURGERS

This traditional example of American fare has now become one of the world's most popular foods – these home-made versions are quick to make and are sure to impress your friends.

Ingredients

1 onion

1 clove of garlic

500 g of minced beef

50 g of breadcrumbs

1 egg

1 tsp of French mustard

Dash of Tabasco sauce

Dash of Worcestershire sauce

Salt

Pepper

Peel and finely chop the onion and garlic, then throw all the ingredients in a bowl and mix together well. Divide the mixture into 4 portions, then shape each portion into something that resembles a burger. Grill for about 4 or 5 minutes on each side under a medium grill, or until golden brown.

Serve in a seeded bun with sliced tomatoes, pickles and a sauce or relish of your choice.

JAMBALAYA

SERVES 4

The sausages that are used in Cajun cooking (native to Louisiana) are different to the British banger. One of the most widely used is the chorizo variety. These are available in the UK, but if you can't find any then ordinary sausages will do. If you don't have (or like) any particular ingredient, be brave and make up your own variation or concoction.

Ingredients

1 onion

2 cloves of garlic

2 chicken breasts

250 g of sausage (chorizo if available)

2 tbsp of olive oil

1 green pepper

2 sticks of celery

Salt

Pepper

1 tsp of cayenne pepper

500 ml of vegetable/chicken stock

250 g of rice

Peel and chop the onion and garlic and cut the chicken and sausage into chunks, then fry them all in the oil in a large saucepan or a wok for about 5 minutes. Deseed and chop the pepper and chop the celery, add to the pan, and continue frying for another couple of minutes, then season and add the cayenne pepper. Pour the stock over the top and bring to the boil.

When the stock is boiling add the rice and cook for roughly 20 minutes or until the rice is soft when pinched.

FISH

Fish are fantastic. Not only are they packed full of goodness, keeping disease at bay and providing you with essential vitamins and nutrients, but the list of ways to cook them is endless. The healthiest method is to bake them, and you can add all sorts of herbs, vegetables or flavourings to bring out their natural, delicate taste. Try your own variations on any of these delicious recipes.

BAKED MACKEREL

SERVES 2

Mackerel also goes well with lemon and herb or other fruity flavours, beetroot, ginger and chilli.

Ingredients

2 mackerel
....

2 tsp of mustard
....

2 tsp of vinegar
....

2 tbsp of water
....

Clean the mackerel, then score across two or three times on each side. Sprinkle with mustard, vinegar and water. Put the fish in a greased baking tin and bake for 15 to 20 minutes at Gas Mark 5 (190 °C, 400 °F).

TOP TIP

You can also cook these fish on the BBQ, in the same way, but keep an eye on them to check when they're cooked.

BAKED FISH IN WINE

SERVES 2

Although the fish in this recipe does need to have a covering of it, it does not need to be swimming in wine. Make sure you save a glass or two to sup with your meal!

Ingredients

2 cod steaks

1 onion

Salt

Pepper

1 glass of wine, red or white

Put the fish in a shallow baking dish. Peel the onion and cut it into rings. Place these on top of the fish, season, pour the wine over the top and bake in the oven for 35 minutes at Gas Mark 5 (190 °C, 375 °F).

TOP TIP

If you use wine in cooking but don't fancy drinking the rest of the bottle that night, you can freeze what's leftover in an ice cube tray, ready to be added to soups or other dishes in future.

KEDGEREE

SERVES 4

This dish is often offered to those convalescing as it is packed full of restorative goodness – a good reason if any to enjoy this wonderful meal.

Ingredients

250 g of smoked haddock fillet

200 g of rice

1 egg

50 g of butter

Juice of 1 lemon

Salt

Pepper

2 tbsp of fresh parsley

Cook the fish by baking it in the oven for 25 minutes. Then remove from the oven, wait for it to cool, then 'flake' the fish, removing all bones and skin. Cook the rice in boiling water according to the instructions on the packet.

Drain and rinse the rice in boiling water – this gets rid of most of the starch. Hard boil the egg by cooking for 10 minutes in boiling water. Then cool, shell and chop into pieces.

Melt the butter in a saucepan and add the fish, and cook for 3 to 4 minutes to reheat it. Stir in the lemon juice, chopped egg, seasoning and rice and serve immediately. Garnish with chopped fresh parsley.

BAKED TROUT

The simplicity of being able to bake this dish in tin foil parcels makes it so appealing, but the ease of the preparation does not take away from the wonderful flavours to be had.

Ingredients

1 onion

1 carrot

1 clove of garlic

15 g of butter

2 small trout

25 g of flaked almonds

Salt

Pepper

Peel and finely chop the onion, carrot and garlic, and fry in the butter in a frying pan for about 5 minutes. Clean each trout and place on a piece of tin foil, making sure the foil is big enough to completely wrap the fish. Divide the vegetables between the two fish, placing them on the top and around the sides of the fish. Sprinkle with the almonds, season, then seal up the 'parcels'.

Bake in the oven for about 20 minutes at Gas Mark 5 (190 °C, 375 °F).

Serve with potatoes, rice or salad.

HADDOCK AND ONION BAKE

This is a healthy and simple dish, that shouldn't take longer than 5 minutes to prepare – all the ingredients of a winner!

Ingredients

1 large onion

4 pieces of haddock

50 g of butter

Salt

Pepper

3 tomatoes

1 tbsp of capers (optional)

Peel the onion and slice it into rings. Put the fish and onion in an ovenproof dish with the butter. Season and bake for 15 minutes at Gas Mark 5 (190 °C, 375 °F). Then add the sliced tomatoes and capers and cook for a further 10 minutes.

Serve with potatoes and fresh vegetables.

TOP TIP

When a recipe calls for onions, you can usually substitute leeks or shallots to vary the taste to your preference.

Student Grub

SKATE WITH SAGE BUTTER

SERVES 2

This is a bit of a treat of a dish because skate can be expensive, but it is very much worth it if you can stretch to it. Look out for good deals at your local fishmonger.

Ingredients

2 tbsp of olive oil

25 g of butter

6 sage leaves

1 large skate wing

2 tsp of capers

Juice of ½ lemon

Salt

Pepper

Heat the oil in a large frying pan (big enough to hold the skate wing), then add the butter and melt. Add the sage leaves and fry gently for 3 minutes, before adding the skate wing. Throw in the capers and lemon juice.

Cook the skate for about 5 minutes on each side, depending on the thickness and season. Serve immediately with all the juices from the pan. Delicious with new potatoes.

SALADS

There are endless recipes for salads, and most people have worked out their own special combinations. Watermelon and feta? Avocado and papaya? Smoked bacon and chilli? Why not!

Not only for the summer months (although local produce will be more readily available and therefore cheaper), a good hearty salad makes a satisfying meal on its own – but you could add a jacket potato or some cous cous to feed especially hungry mouths. Here are some of my favourite recipes.

ALSACE SALAD

 SERVES 2

This is one of my favourite salads, which brings a taste of both France and Germany to the mix and offers robustness to a light lunch.

Ingredients

4 rashers of bacon

2 tbsp of oil

2 eggs

1 lettuce

2 tomatoes

Salt

Pepper

Cut the bacon rashers into pieces, and fry in the oil. With this particular recipe the bacon pieces need to be verging on crispness, but don't let them burn. When they are cooked, put them aside in a separate dish or bowl. Clear the pan of any debris then fry the eggs. Whilst the eggs are cooking arrange the lettuce leaves in a serving dish with the quartered tomatoes and the bacon. When the eggs are cooked let them cool for a minute and then place on top of the salad, then season.

TOP TIP

If you want to keep your lettuce crisp and fresh, place in a sealed plastic bag along with a damp paper towel. The towel will absorb any moisture, preventing the lettuce from wilting and going soggy.

ITALIAN PEPPER SALAD

There are many ways of serving peppers but this simple recipe is one of the best.

Ingredients

4 large peppers (mixture of colours)

1 tsp of capers

4 tbsp of olive oil

Salt

Pepper

Heat the oven to the highest setting possible, and then place the whole peppers on a tray on the top shelf. They should stay in the oven for 20 to 30 minutes after the oven is up to temperature. After about 15 minutes turn the peppers over so they are evenly cooked.

Remove from the oven and put the peppers in a clean polythene bag and tie closed, or use any airtight container – this helps to 'steam' them and loosen the skin. Leave the peppers in the container for at least 15 minutes then remove and peel off the skins. Make sure all the skin is removed, as when it is burnt it has a very strong flavour and can taint the dish.

After removing the skin, remove the stems and seeds then cut into strips. Place the peppers in a serving dish with the capers, drizzle with the oil and then season. There will normally be some residue from the peppers in the polythene bag that can be added to the dish for extra flavour. To add extra healthy goodness, try serving it on a large bed of salad leaves.

CUCUMBER SALAD

Cucumbers are very high in water content, which is great for your skin and to help you digest those heavier meals. They make a super-refreshing salad.

Ingredients

1 large cucumber
Salt
1 tbsp of white wine vinegar
1 tbsp of olive oil
1 tsp of sugar
Pepper
2 tbsp of fresh chives

Peel the cucumber and slice as thinly as possible. A mandolin is ideal for producing wafer-thin slices, but a potato peeler will do the job just as well.

Arrange the slices of cucumber on a flat plate and sprinkle generously with salt. Place another plate of a similar size on top and press down gently.

Leave in the fridge for 1 hour, then pour away the water that has been extracted. Mix the vinegar, oil and sugar together, then pour over the cucumber. Season, then sprinkle with the chopped chives.

PASTA SALAD

A simple and colourful salad with an Italian feel.

Ingredients

100 g of pasta quills or shells

185 g tin of tuna

1 red pepper

3 tomatoes

Salt

Pepper

French dressing (optional)

Cook the pasta according to the instructions on the packet, then drain.

Drain the oil from the tuna. Deseed and chop the red pepper, and slice the tomatoes, then mix all of the ingredients in a serving bowl. Add 2 to 3 tablespoons of dressing if desired.

See p.38 for a recipe for French dressing.

RICE AND SWEETCORN

This is a simple, sweet salad, which is surprisingly satisfying.

Ingredients

200 g or 1 cup of rice

1 green pepper

4 tomatoes

225 g tin of sweetcorn

Salt

Pepper

French dressing

Wash the rice in a sieve to remove some of the starch. Put the rice in a large saucepan with about half a litre of water and a pinch of salt. After the water has boiled, simmer for about 20 to 25 minutes or until the rice is tender, then drain well. Chop and deseed the pepper and chop the tomatoes. Mix all the ingredients with the rice and pour a little French dressing (see recipe on p.38) on top.

SALADE NIÇOISE

There has long been a raging debate over what makes the perfect salade Niçoise: tuna or anchovies? Olives or green beans? We say, throw it all in and enjoy the delicious taste of them all combined! This recipe traditionally uses tuna steak, but you get the same taste from a tin and for a fraction of the price.

Ingredients

2 eggs

150 g of French beans

1 lettuce

3 tomatoes

185 g tin of tuna

French dressing

10 black olives

6 anchovy fillets

Salt

Pepper

Hard boil the eggs for 8 minutes, then place in a bowl of cold water. Add the beans for the last few minutes to cook them through. Wash the lettuce and place the leaves in a large serving bowl, then add the tuna (drain the oil first) and toss it all together.

Quarter the tomatoes and place them on top of the lettuce. Shell the eggs, cut them into quarters, and arrange them neatly on top. Pour the dressing over the salad (see recipe on p.38), and add the olives, beans and anchovies, if desired. Season.

TOMATO AND ONION

A typical Provençal salad – and a classic combination of flavours.

Ingredients

1 red onion

4 fresh tomatoes

Fresh basil

Salt

Pepper

French dressing

Peel the onion and slice fairly thinly. Slice the tomatoes and arrange them on a large plate or dish. Place the onion pieces between the tomato slices. Decorate with the basil leaves, and season well. Pour the French dressing over the top (see recipe on p.38).

POTATO SALAD

SERVES 2

Chopped fresh chives or coriander makes a great finishing touch to this British picnic staple.

Ingredients

6 medium-sized new potatoes

25 g of butter

Mayonnaise

Salt

Pepper

If you don't have new potatoes and want to use old ones (not quite the same flavour but a close enough alternative), you must peel them first. Place the potatoes in boiling water for 15 minutes or until a knife will pass through the centre fairly easily. Drain, then cut into 2.5 cm cubes and place in a bowl with the butter. When the potatoes have cooled add a good coating of mayonnaise. Mix together and season.

Chopped fresh chives, coriander or lemon juice can be added if you like. If you are using small new potatoes they can be left whole. Another alternative to using mayonnaise is to place new potatoes in a bowl with a couple of tablespoons of olive oil.

AVOCADO SALAD

The luxurious taste of avocados can turn an ordinary salad into something truly succulent. This superfood is bursting with healthy vitamins and minerals, making this a perfect pick-me-up after an indulgent weekend. When choosing an avocado to be eaten straight away make sure it is ripe – it should be slightly soft when the skin is pressed.

Ingredients

1 avocado

6 cherry tomatoes

½ of a red onion

French dressing

Remove the skin of the avocado using a knife. Then cut in half, around the stone in the middle, then pull the two halves away from each other. The stone will stay lodged in one side. The easiest way of removing the stone is to stick a sharp knife in it and then ease it out.

After removing the stone, cut the avocado into slices. Cut the cherry tomatoes in half, and peel and finely slice the red onion into rings. Toss together and cover with French dressing (see recipe on p.38). You could try variations of this salad by adding salad leaves, cous cous, cooked bacon or mango.

TABBOULEH

SERVES 4

Bulghur wheat is widely used in countries like Morocco and Tunisia. You can substitute it with cous cous, if you prefer – just reduce the boiling time by 10 minutes. This fragrant salad is full of green goodness.

Ingredients

150 g of bulghur wheat

1 bunch of parsley

1 bunch of spring onions

½ cucumber

1 tomato

8 mint leaves

4 tbsp of olive oil

Juice of 1 lemon

Salt

Pepper

Place the bulghur wheat in a saucepan of water. Bring to the boil, then simmer gently for 10 to 15 minutes until tender. Drain, then allow to cool.

Finely chop the parsley, spring onions, cucumber, tomato and mint leaves, and toss together with the bulghur in a serving bowl. Add the olive oil, lemon juice, salt and pepper. Mix together thoroughly and serve.

SMOKED SALMON SALAD

*Although smoked salmon is not exactly a 'budget' food, a little goes a long way –
and your friends will definitely be impressed with this sophisticated dish!*

Ingredients

Salad leaves

100 g of smoked salmon

1 lemon

Olive oil

Salt

Pepper

Cut the salmon into small pieces. Toss together with the salad leaves (rocket and spinach leaves work well, giving it a lovely peppery taste), olive oil, salt and a little pepper. Serve with the lemon, cut into wedges.

SNACKS AND MIDNIGHT CRAVINGS

This is another essential section; when breakfast or lunch is skipped a snack can keep the hunger at bay until the evening meal. It is interesting to compare what people regard as a 'snack': for some it is a plate of chips, a pile of sandwiches and a couple of doughnuts, while for others it could be half an apple.

B.L.T.

Otherwise known as a bacon, lettuce and tomato sandwich. Note that this is not your everyday type of sarnie – this is heading towards the realms of haute cuisine!

Ingredients

2 rashers of bacon

3 slices of bread

Butter

Handful of lettuce leaves

1 tomato

Salt

Pepper

Grill the bacon and the bread (the bacon will take longer though, so keep an eye on both!). Once the bread has toasted, spread it with butter, then place a bit of lettuce, some slices of tomato and a rasher of bacon on it. Put a slice of toast on top and then make up another layer as before. Finish with the last piece of toast on top, then cut diagonally across. Add a dash of salt, pepper and a little mayonnaise to the insides if required.

To stop the B.L.T. from falling apart you could try skewering it with a cocktail stick. But under no circumstances should you swallow the cocktail stick in your haste to eat your masterpiece – they are not particularly palatable.

BACON AND CHEESE SANDWICH

SERVES 1

This for me is the ultimate sandwich… simple, but devastating.

Ingredients

2 rashers of bacon

Butter

2 slices of bread

Cheddar cheese

Tomato sauce

Grill the bacon for a couple of minutes on each side, longer if you prefer it crispy. Whilst the bacon is grilling, butter the bread and cut a few slices of cheese. When the bacon is cooked place between the slices of bread with the cheese, then squirt some tomato sauce inside – lovely.

TOP TIP

To stop bacon from curling when cooking, simply dip the rashers into cold water before you place them in the pan or grill.

POOR MAN'S PASTA

SERVES 1

There are few recipes that are this simple yet taste this good. A perfect dish to repel a hunger attack, and it only takes a few minutes to prepare.

Ingredients

100 g of pasta

2 tbsp of olive oil

½ clove of garlic

Salt

Pepper

Cook the pasta according to the instructions on the packet. When the pasta is cooked, drain and place in a small serving bowl. Using the saucepan you cooked the pasta in heat the oil, peel and finely chop the garlic, and fry gently for a minute. Pour the oil over the pasta and mix. Season. If you wish to make it a little more exciting add grated cheese on top or a finely chopped small red chilli in with the garlic, but remove the seeds first if you don't want it too hot.

HAM AND EGGS

This is a perfect supper dish, tastier than your average British cafe grub and healthier too.

Ingredients

1 tin of chopped tomatoes

4 slices of thick-cut ham

4 eggs

2 tsp of oregano

Salt

Pepper

Heat the oven to its maximum temperature. Pour the tomatoes into a baking dish then roll up the slices of ham and place on top of the tomatoes. Break the eggs carefully on top of the ham, sprinkle with the oregano and season. Bake until the eggs are cooked.

Serve with hot buttered toast and a freshly prepared salad, or steamed vegetables.

WELSH RAREBIT

Doesn't taste particularly Welsh, nor is it very rare. But there's no doubt that it's delicious.

Ingredients

150 g of Cheddar cheese

15 g of butter

½ tsp of dry mustard

2 tbsp of flour

4 rashers of streaky bacon

2 slices of bread

Grate the cheese and put into a small saucepan. Add the butter and mustard, then cook gently, stirring constantly, until the cheese has melted. Take the saucepan away from the heat and add the flour, beating it in until smooth. Allow to cool.

Grill the bacon and the bread (keeping an eye on them to make sure they don't burn), then spread the cheese mixture evenly over the toast. Grill until golden, then add the bacon and serve.

For a more traditional rarebit, you could add ale (or cider) when melting the cheese, and spread the toast with Worcestershire sauce before spreading the cheese mixture on top.

PLAIN OMELETTE

A really easy way to use up eggs, or knock together a quick and filling snack.

Ingredients

2 or 3 eggs
Pinch of mixed herbs
Salt
Pepper
25 g of butter

Beat the eggs together in a mixing bowl and add the seasoning. Melt the butter in a frying pan and pour in the eggs.

As soon as the eggs start to cook, lift up one edge of the omelette with a spatula, tilt the pan and let the uncooked egg run underneath. Continue to do this until the omelette is cooked, then flip it in half and serve on a warmed plate.

To add interest, you could try one of these variations:

Cheese and Tomato

Prepare as above, but add 50 g grated cheese and 1 chopped tomato before pouring into the frying pan.

Bacon

Cut 2 rashers of bacon up into little pieces and fry for a couple of minutes, then add to the mixture and follow the instructions above.

EGG AND CHEESE RAMEKINS

SERVES 1

Ingredients

1 tsp of butter

50 g of cheese

1 tomato

1 egg

Salt

Pepper

Using the butter grease a small ovenproof dish, preferably a ramekin dish or one that is about 7.5 cm in diameter. Put grated cheese in the bottom of the dish (Cheddar is ideal, but you could also try Red Leicester or Edam) and up the sides. Place a slice of tomato inside and then the egg, trying not to break the yolk. Add the seasoning and cover with another slice of tomato and more grated cheese.

Bake in the oven for about 15 minutes at Gas Mark 4 (180 °C, 350 °F) or until the egg is set. You can then either eat it straight out of the ramekin or, if you feel it is well enough set, turn it out onto a plate.

You could also try adding in slices of mushroom instead of or as well as the tomato.

POTATO, BACON AND ONION FRY

SERVES 4

These patties are a slightly more creative way to prepare bacon than the B.L.T., but they're just as mouth-watering.

Ingredients

1 onion

500 g of potatoes

4 rashers of bacon

2 eggs

1 tbsp of plain flour

Salt

Pepper

2 tbsp of vegetable oil

Peel the onion and potatoes, then coarsely grate them and place in a mixing bowl. Chop the bacon into small pieces and add to the bowl, along with the beaten eggs and flour. Mix together, then season. Heat the oil in a frying pan, then add heaped tablespoons of the mixture into the pan to form small circles. Fry the potato cakes on both sides till they turn a golden brown. Continue doing this until all the mixture is used up.

Serve with baked beans or a salad.

BREAKFAST TIME AND SMOOTHIES

Breakfast is the most important meal of the day, but it is all too often rushed or ignored altogether. On lecture days you may not wake up early enough to make some of these recipes, but smoothies can be made in advance and frozen or refrigerated, and on your days off why not indulge in French toast, a luxurious porridge or a protein-packed poached egg?

EGGS

Eaten in moderation, eggs can be very healthy – they are a great source of protein, amino acids and even vitamin D, and are even said to help prevent cancer, blood clots and stroke. Even better – they taste great no matter how you prepare them.

Scrambled

SERVES 2

One of the most interesting ways of cooking eggs, as you can add anything you like to the mixture – try onions, garlic, herbs, ham, or cheese.

Ingredients

3 eggs

4 tbsp of milk

Pepper

25 g of butter

Whisk the eggs in a bowl and add the milk and pepper. Melt the butter in a saucepan and add the egg mixture. Stir the mixture continuously as it thickens. Don't have the heat up too high, or else the egg will burn and stick to the pan.

Serve on top of hot, buttered toast.

Poached

One of the healthiest methods for cooking eggs as it requires no cooking fat or oil.

Ingredients

1 egg per person

The traditional way of poaching eggs is to boil some water in a saucepan and then, after breaking the egg into a cup or mug, slide it gently into the water. Only put one egg in at a time, and wait for it to firm up before removing with a slotted spoon. An alternative is to use cling film to line a ramekin, crack the egg on top, and then close up the edges of the cling to create an airtight pouch. You can then put this in the boiling water without fear of your egg breaking and making a gooey mess of your best saucepan.

Boiled

Quick, easy, healthy… and you can dunk toasty soldiers in them too. What more could you ask for?

Ingredients

1 egg per person

1 slice of bread per person

Boil some water in a saucepan and carefully lower the egg, whole, into the water, using a spoon. Then boil for 3 to 4 minutes, depending on how runny you want the egg to be.

After removing the egg from the water, whack the top with a spoon – this will stop the egg from hardening. Meanwhile, toast a slice of bread and cut into long thin strips. Dunk them into the runny egg and enjoy!

If you require the egg to be hard boiled, cook for about 8 minutes in boiling water.

If your egg cracks whilst it is cooking, pouring a tablespoon of vinegar in the water will help seal it.

Fried

Perfect with sausages and hash browns.

Ingredients

1 egg per person

2 tbsp of oil

Heat some oil in a frying pan, but don't let the fat get too hot or the egg will stick to the pan and bubble. Crack the egg on the side of the pan and plop the egg into the oil. Fry gently for about 3 minutes, basting occasionally and lifting the edges with a spatula as they cook to prevent sticking. If you like your eggs American-style (over-easy), fry both sides of the egg.

FRENCH TOAST

SERVES 2

This is a wonderfully indulgent and versatile recipe. Try topping it with sliced bananas, chocolate sauce, maple syrup, caramelised peaches, or strawberry jam.

Ingredients

4 eggs

1 cup of milk

1 tsp of sugar

1 tsp of salt

Butter

Slices of bread without the crusts

Beat the eggs and the milk together and add the sugar and salt. Heat a knob of butter in a frying pan. Dip a slice of bread in the egg mixture and then heat slowly for a couple of minutes on each side until golden brown. Serve hot with your choice of toppings.

PORRIDGE

The perfect start to a cold wintry day – nutritious, warming and tasty.

Ingredients

100 g of oatmeal

100 ml of milk

300 ml of boiling water

Salt

Mix the oatmeal and milk into a paste and add boiling water. Heat and simmer in a saucepan for 15 minutes, stirring occasionally. Stir in a pinch of salt and serve with syrup, jam or fruit.

SMOOTHIES

For those of you who can't quite manage food at breakfast time or are in need of a quick, healthy energy boost, here's a selection of delicious smoothies. You will need a blender or smoothie maker for these recipes.

Breakfast Smoothie

This is wonderfully filling and tastes so good you'd be forgiven for forgetting how healthy it actually is.

Ingredients

1 large banana

200 ml of milk

2 tbsp of rolled porridge oats

2 tsp of runny honey

2 ice cubes

Place all of the ingredients into the blender and blend until smooth.

BREAKFAST TIME AND SMOOTHIES

Strawberry Smoothie

Perfect for those who prefer a lighter start to the day. You could try experimenting with different fruits and juices – use whatever is in season to save the planet as well as your pennies.

Ingredients

½ Cantaloupe melon

10 strawberries

240 ml of orange juice

4 ice cubes

Peel the melon, remove the seeds and cube the flesh. Wash the strawberries thoroughly and cut off the green leafy tops. Place all of the ingredients into the blender and blend until smooth.

Banana and Raspberry Smoothie

This tropical smoothie is one of the most refreshing combinations you could ask for. If you want to make it really exotic, try adding coconut milk or dessicated coconut.

Ingredients

2 bananas

240 ml of pineapple juice

120 ml of natural yogurt

175 g of raspberries

4 ice cubes

Place all of the ingredients into the blender and blend until smooth.

Mango, Strawberry and Banana Smoothie

Try adding a sprinkling of rolled oats or muesli on top to make this a more substantial breakfast.

Ingredients

5 strawberries

100 g of mango flesh

1 small banana

200 ml of apple juice

Wash the strawberries carefully and cut off the green leafy tops. Peel and chop the mango. Place all of the ingredients into the blender and blend until smooth.

Kiwi and Melon Smoothie

Zingy and sweet, super-healthy and refreshing – the perfect smoothie!

Ingredients

½ honeydew melon

1 kiwi fruit

1 apple

2 tsp of honey

4 ice cubes

Peel and slice the melon and kiwi fruit. Peel the apple and core it, then cut into small chunks. Place all of the ingredients into the blender and blend until smooth.

COOKIES AND CAKES

Home-made cakes and cookies are so much nicer than the shop-bought, additive-laden varieties. Here is a selection of yummy recipes, great for special occasions or for when you and your friends just want to indulge.

CHOCOLATE BROWNIES

There's nothing more mouth-watering than warm chocolate brownies with a big scoop of real vanilla ice cream.

Ingredients

150 g of unsalted butter

200 g of dark chocolate

2 eggs

200 g of dark muscovado sugar

100 g of plain flour

1 tsp of baking powder

Grease an 18 cm square cake tin with a little of the butter and line with non-stick baking parchment (or greaseproof paper). Break the chocolate into pieces and place with the butter in a heatproof bowl over a pan of simmering water. Don't let the water boil, or else the water will spill over. Stir the chocolate and butter mixture together with a spoon. Beat the eggs and sugar together in a separate bowl using a handheld mixer if you have one, or by hand if you don't. Add in the melted chocolate and butter, and then the flour and baking powder. Stir thoroughly.

Pour the mixture into the tin and bake for 30 minutes, at Gas Mark 3 (160 °C, 325 °F). Allow to cool for 10 minutes before cutting into squares.

VICTORIA SPONGE

This British teatime classic is well worth making the effort for – and it's sure to go down a treat at any occasion.

Ingredients

150 g of butter
....
150 g of caster sugar
....
3 eggs
....
150 g of self-raising flour
....
Jam
....

Grease two 18 cm sandwich tins with a knob of the butter. Mix together the sugar and butter until they are smooth in texture. Gradually add the eggs to the mixture, then fold in the flour. Divide the mixture between the two baking tins. Make sure that the tops of the cakes are level, then bake in the oven for 20 to 25 minutes at Gas Mark 5 (190 °C, 375 °F).

To see if it is cooked, stick a skewer or a knitting needle (if you don't happen to have either to hand then a knife will do) into the centre of the sponge. If bits of the mixture are stuck to it when it is drawn out, the cake needs to be cooked a little longer. If the skewer comes out clean, the cake is ready.

Now turn the cakes out of the tins onto a wire rack (use an oven rack if you don't have one specifically for cakes). Once completely cooled, spread your favourite jam over one of the layers, sandwich the other one on top, and sprinkle with caster sugar.

ICED CHOCOLATE CAKE

This double chocolate cake is truly indulgent, the perfect celebration cake.

Ingredients

150 g of butter

150 g of caster sugar

3 eggs

150 g of self-raising flour

40 g of cocoa

1½ tbsp of water

For the icing:

100 g of plain cooking chocolate

40 g of butter

200 g of icing sugar

2 tbsp of warm water

Grease two 18 cm sandwich tins with a knob of the butter. Place the sugar and the butter in a large mixing bowl and mix together, using either a wooden spoon or an electric mixer if you have one. Add the eggs, one at a time, and beat together.

In a separate bowl, mix the flour and the cocoa powder together, then add it to the creamed mixture. Continue mixing, adding water until a soft dropping consistency is achieved. Divide the mixture equally between the two sandwich tins. Bake in the oven at Gas Mark 5 (190 °C, 375 °F) for 25 to 30 minutes.

Test the cake by inserting a skewer into it. If the mixture sticks to it, the cake needs a few more minutes in the oven.

When the cakes are ready, turn them out of their tins onto a wire rack. Melt the chocolate by breaking it into squares and placing it in a basin, then putting that over the top of a saucepan of boiling water. Be careful not to let the water boil over the top of the saucepan into the chocolate.

After the chocolate has melted, allow to cool. Cream together the butter and half the icing sugar, then add half the melted chocolate. Mix, and spread over one side of the cake, then sandwich the two together.

The rest of the chocolate is used to make the icing on the top. Add the water and remaining icing sugar to the chocolate and mix thoroughly, then spoon onto the top of the cake. Spread the icing around using a palette knife that has been dipped in hot water (this helps to spread the icing and stop it sticking to the knife). You can then let your imagination run wild with the decorations – supermarkets stock whole ranges of cake toppings, from those little silver balls to miniature marzipan people.

TOP TIP

Use wholewheat flour instead of white to make these cakes healthier. If you're not so keen on the taste, just replace half the amount with wholewheat to get the best of both!

LOW-FAT BANANA MUFFINS

Not all cakes have to be sugar-laden and fatty – these tasty treats will make you feel that eating cake can actually be good for you.

Ingredients

125 g of plain flour

50 g of light brown sugar

½ tsp of bicarbonate of soda

1 tsp of baking powder

½ tsp of ground cinnamon

100 g of rolled oats

2 eggs

2 tbsp of vegetable oil

3 medium bananas

125 ml of buttermilk

Prepare a 12-hole muffin tin with either paper liners or a thin coating of oil.

Place the flour, sugar, bicarbonate, baking powder, cinnamon and oats into a large bowl and mix well.

In another bowl beat the eggs, then add the oil. Mash the bananas and add, along with the buttermilk, then combine. Fold this mixture into the flour mixture, and stir thoroughly. Divide the mixture between the muffin cups and bake for 20 minutes at Gas Mark 6 (200 °C, 400 °F).

Leave to cool for 10 minutes in the tin, then turn out onto a wire rack.

GRANDMA'S CHOCOLATE CHIP COOKIES

This is one of my grandmother's recipes. I would like to thank her for the regular supply of these cookies throughout my formative years.

Ingredients

75 g of butter

75 g of granulated sugar

25 g of brown sugar

1 egg

2 drops of vanilla essence

100 g of cooking chocolate

150 g of self-raising flour

Grease a flat baking tray with a knob of butter. Cream the butter and the sugars either in a mixer or with a wooden spoon. Beat in the egg and vanilla. Grate or chop the chocolate coarsely, then stir into the creamed mixture along with the flour. Using a teaspoon place balls of the mixture on the baking tray, spaced well apart as they spread as they cook. Bake in the centre of the oven for about 15 minutes at Gas Mark 5 (190 °C, 375 °F). Place on a wire tray and leave until cold.

Uncooked cookie dough can be frozen for up to three months, or kept in the fridge for three days.

FLAPJACKS

For those with access to two baking trays and living in a large household it can be advisable to double the quantities given here, as flapjacks tend to disappear fast!

Ingredients

100 g of butter

4 tbsp of golden syrup

75 g of sugar

Pinch of salt

200 g of porridge oats

Grease a shallow baking tray with a knob of butter. Melt the butter in a large saucepan, then add the syrup and leave over a low heat for a couple of minutes, stirring continuously. Remove from the heat and add the sugar, salt and oats. Mix thoroughly using a wooden spoon, making sure all the oats are covered with syrup.

Spoon the mixture evenly into the baking try, and cook for 20 to 30 minutes at Gas Mark 4 (180 ºC, 350 ºF). Cut the flapjacks into bars before they cool.

SCONES

Ingredients

200 g of self-raising flour

Pinch of salt

50 g of butter

125 ml of milk

Sift the flour into a large mixing bowl through a sieve (if you don't have one, it's not the end of the world, but it really helps to make the scones light). Mix in the salt. Cut the butter into small cubes and add them to the flour. Rub the mixture between your fingers until the result looks like breadcrumbs.

Add the milk and stir in using the blade of a knife to form a soft dough. Roll out the mixture on a floured board until it is about 1.5 cm thick. Cut into rounds using a biscuit cutter or a glass.

Grease a baking tray and place some scones on it, leaving big enough gaps for them to rise. Brush some milk over the top of the scones to obtain a smooth and shiny finish.

Bake in the oven for 10 to 15 minutes at Gas Mark 7 (210 °C, 425 °F).

You could also try these easy variations:

Cheese Scones

Follow the directions for plain scones, but stir in 100 g of grated Cheddar cheese before adding the milk.

Fruit Scones

Follow the directions for plain scones, but stir in 25 g of sugar and 50 g of dried fruit, sultanas, currants, etc. before baking.

PUDDINGS

There's nothing more comforting than a nice hot pud after dinner, especially on cold, dark evenings. Shop-bought puddings pale in comparison to these delights, and these are all perfect for sharing with friends and housemates.

TREACLE TART

This can be served hot or cold, with cream or ice cream or just on its own. Simply delicious.

Ingredients

100 g of plain flour

Pinch of salt

50 g of butter

3 tbsp of water

12 tbsp of golden syrup

50 g of fresh white breadcrumbs

2 tsp of grated lemon rind

Sieve the flour and add the salt. Cut the butter into small pieces and rub them into the flour until the mixture resembles fine breadcrumbs. Add a tablespoon of water at a time until a firm dough is produced. Cover a clean surface or pastry board with a sprinkling of flour. Roll out the pastry so that there is enough to cover the bottom and the sides of a 20 cm flan dish, trimming away any excess with a knife. Mix the syrup, breadcrumbs and lemon rind together well, then spoon into the flan case. Bake for about 25 minutes at Gas Mark 6 (200 °C, 400 °F) until golden.

CROISSANT PUDDING

Once you introduce this sinful treat to your friends they're bound to demand it again and again.

Ingredients

5 croissants

Butter

2 egg yolks

50 g of caster sugar

300 ml of milk

300 ml of double cream

2 drops of vanilla essence

50 g of raisins

Ground cinnamon

Brown sugar

Cut the croissants lengthways and cut in half. Butter one side of the croissants and put to one side. Beat the egg yolks, caster sugar, milk, cream and vanilla essence, then put aside. Grease an ovenproof dish with a knob of butter and place a layer of croissants on the bottom, then sprinkle with raisins. Continue layering until all the croissants are used up.

Briefly beat the milk mixture, then pour over the croissants. Sprinkle with cinnamon. Leave to soak for at least 30 minutes.

Whilst the croissants are soaking, preheat the oven to Gas Mark 4 (180 °C, 350 °F).

Sprinkle a thin layer of brown sugar over the top of the dish. Put the dish in a deep-sided baking tray and pour boiling water into the tin, roughly halfway up to the side of the dish, making sure it doesn't spill over into the cake dish. Cook in the middle of the oven for 40 minutes.

BAKED BANANAS

A tasty way to get one of your five a day – and super-quick and easy to make, too.

Ingredients

1 banana per person

Brown or golden granulated sugar

Lemon juice

Preheat the oven to Gas Mark 4 (180 °C, 350 °F). Peel the banana and place it on a large piece of foil, shiny side uppermost. Squeeze the lemon juice over the banana, sprinkle with brown sugar, and loosely wrap the foil around it. Place in the centre of the oven on a baking tray and cook until soft to the touch (around 15 to 20 minutes).

For a slightly more decadent alternative, replace the sugar and lemon juice with chocolate buttons to create your own warm and delicious chocolate sauce. Serve with cream or ice cream.

BAKED APPLES

This healthy pud has stood the test of time, and is a favourite with kids and adults alike. If you don't have mincemeat, try making your own with raisins, currants and sultanas mixed with the brown sugar and plenty of cinnamon.

Ingredients

1 large cooking apple per person

Mincemeat

Brown sugar

Butter

Remove the cores from the apples and stand them in an ovenproof dish. Fill the hole in the apple with mincemeat and a teaspoon of brown sugar. Add a knob of butter on top. Put enough water in the dish to cover the bottom of the apples. Bake at Gas Mark 4 (180 °C, 350 °F) for about an hour. Test the apple with a skewer; it should be soft, but not too soft. Serve with cream or a scoop of vanilla ice cream.

RASPBERRY BRÛLÉE

SERVES 4

Traditionally brûlées are finished off with a kitchen blowtorch. Thankfully, this method is far safer and is guaranteed to produce a perfect pud.

Ingredients

250 g of fresh raspberries

250 ml of double cream

150 g of demerara or golden granulated sugar

Place the raspberries in a shallow heatproof dish. Whip the cream until thick, (but not too stiff) and spread over the raspberries. Sprinkle the sugar over the cream, covering it completely.

Place under the preheated grill until it is dark and bubbling.

Remove from the grill and leave to cool, then chill in the fridge for a couple of hours.

If raspberries are out of season or are too pricey, an equally tasty version can be made using sliced banana.

PLUM CRUMBLE

SERVES 4

A lovely simple dish, which tastes great whichever in-season fruit you use.

Ingredients

8 ripe plums

2 tbsp of water

50 g of sugar

A pinch of cinnamon

100 g of plain flour

100 g of butter

50 g of rolled oats

Cut the plums into quarters, removing the stones, then place in a large ovenproof dish. Sprinkle over the water, two tablespoons of the sugar and then the cinnamon. Put the flour in a mixing bowl then cut the butter into small cubes and add to the bowl. Using your fingertips rub the two ingredients together until they resemble large breadcrumbs. Add the remaining sugar and oats and mix together.

Spoon the crumble mixture over the plums until evenly covered. Bake for 45 minutes at Gas Mark 6 (200 °C, 400 °F). Serve hot with custard or cream.

PANCAKES

Although they are traditionally made on Shrove Tuesday to use up larder ingredients before Lent, I'm a firm believer that pancakes make a great treat any day of the year.

Ingredients

100 g of plain flour

Pinch of salt

1 egg

250 ml of milk

Butter or oil

Put the flour and salt in a bowl and add the egg into the middle. Pour in about a third of the milk. Stir gently, adding the rest of milk a little at a time. Beat the mixture thoroughly, then pour into a jug.

Melt a small knob of butter in a frying pan or heat a few drops of oil, then add a couple of tablespoons of the batter. Tip the frying pan to spread the mixture evenly. Fry until the underside is brown, using a spatula to lift the edges so that they don't stick, then toss the pancake (or, if there's no one around to impress, you could flip the pancake using a spatula or palette knife).

Tip the finished pancake onto a plate and cover with lemon juice and sugar, or maple syrup.

PINEAPPLE IN BATTER

This is a nice and easy pud, and tastes wonderful when served hot with custard.

Ingredients

100 g of plain flour

Pinch of salt

1 egg

250 ml of milk

1 tin of pineapple rings

2 tbsp of oil

Prepare the mixture as with the pancakes, then dip a pineapple ring in the batter and fry in the oil until it turns golden brown. You could also use sliced bananas.

FRESH FRUIT SALAD

SERVES 4

Not even a hint of chocolate.

Ingredients

1 banana

2 oranges

1 apple

1 pear

50 g of grapes

100 g of strawberries

Juice of 1 lemon

2 tbsp of sugar

150 ml of water

The above ingredients are just a guide. You can use any fruit that is available or affordable. Wash all fruit before starting. Put the lemon juice and sugar in a bowl and mix together.

Cut the apple into quarters, remove the core and chop into small pieces.

Peel the oranges using a sharp knife, making sure all the pips are removed. Cut into segments, cutting between the membranes.

Cut the grapes in half and remove any pips. Peel the banana and cut into slices.

Skin and quarter the pear, then core it and chop into small pieces. The strawberries should be hulled (remove the leafy green bit at the top), and cut in half.

Put all the fruit in the bowl with the lemon juice, sugar, and water, and mix thoroughly.

Serve either on its own or with cream. If you're not eating it straight away or have leftovers, store in an airtight container in the fridge, covered in the syrup.

COFFEES

If you are a fan of the big-name coffee companies but don't want to pay the high prices, here are a few coffee recipes to try – they make a great alternative to the instant stuff and will really impress your friends. Basic utensils required are a coffee pot and blender.

WHITE MOCHA

SERVES 6

Hot, rich, creamy and chocolatey. Need I say more?

Ingredients

75 g of white chocolate

2 cups of milk

2 cups of hot coffee

Whipped cream

Grate the chocolate and heat with the milk in a saucepan. Stir with a wooden spoon until melted and smooth. Stir in the hot coffee (either instant or the real thing, depending on how strong you like it) and serve with whipped cream and a sprinkling of the white chocolate on top.

BLACK FOREST COFFEE

SERVES 1

This is almost a dessert in itself, very simple to make but strictly for those with a sweet tooth.

Ingredients

150 ml of hot coffee

2 tbsp of chocolate syrup

1 tbsp of cherry juice (maraschino or morello)

Cherries (maraschino or morello)

Whipped cream

Chocolate shavings

Mix the coffee, chocolate syrup and cherry juice in a cup. Top with whipped cream, then, removing any stones from cherries (if they are fresh), sprinkle them on top along with the chocolate shavings.

AMARETTO ICED COFFEE

SERVES 6

You'll feel like you're sitting on the veranda of an Italian cafe soaking up the sun with this wonderfully refreshing, sweet treat.

Ingredients

3 cups of cold coffee

2 cups of vanilla ice cream

1 cup of milk

¼ cup of Amaretto

2 tsp of vanilla

1 tsp of almond extract

4 ice cubes

Combine all of the ingredients in a blender and whip until smooth. Half-fill six glasses with crushed ice and top up with the coffee mixture.

CONCLUSION

So, you are now a well-travelled (gastronomically speaking) student cook, and are probably full from trying so many wonderful recipes. The only thing to do now is to remember that these recipes should remain part of your diet after you leave uni and are forced to discover the real world. Life will get tough, pressures will increase, the daily dose of stress will become as common as the daily sessions of *Hollyoaks* are now, but deep down you will know that when you get home you will be able to cook a fine meal. Whatever happens, I hope this book has been as entertaining as it has been useful, and that after reading it your housemates will be astounded by your newly acquired culinary skill and imagination.

Bon appétit!

Have you enjoyed this book?
If so, why not write a review on your favourite website?

If you're interested in finding out more about our books, find us on Facebook at **Summersdale Publishers** and follow us on Twitter at **@Summersdale**.

Thanks very much for buying this Summersdale book.

www.summersdale.com